PRA

MW01035328

"*Copyrighteous* will surprise you. It's not just a book about using resources responsibly and attributing. It's an inspiring encouragement to forge your own path, tap into your creativity and create the class of your dreams. As a proud textbook ditcher, this book spoke to my teacher soul!"

—**Matt Miller**, *author of* Ditch That Textbook, *blogger, speaker, and veteran educator*

"This is the book that educators have been waiting for, even if they didn't realize it was what they needed! *Copyrighteous* by Diana Gill is so much more than a framework about doing what's best for kids and teachers when citing sources and creating content.

"Diana uses a very personal approach, telling stories from her own experience and incorporating her children that will engage readers of all levels and make them better educators in the process. This book is a must-read for you and your entire school!"

—**Adam Welcome**, *educator, speaker, author, and runner, family*

"In her new book, *Copyrighteous,* author and educator Diana Gill gives voice to teaching and learning with the perfect blend of personal stories and instructional best practice. Sharing truth with humor, Gill provides educators the tools to allow creativity to legally transform the curriculum."

—**Candice Dodson**, *executive director, SETDA*

"Told from a place of understanding and compassion, Diana Gill uses personal anecdotes and field experience in *Copyrighteous* to help us all become better sharers, creators, and professionals."

—**Jen Giffen**, *teacher-librarian and edtech specialist, Richmond Hill, Ontario, Canada*

"Diana has managed to create a book about copyright that cuts right to the heart of what it takes to bring out the best teacher within all of us. *Copyrighteous* is an inspiring look at how we can take potential hurdles and turn them into launching pads to create rich and engaging learning experiences for our students."

—**Jesse Lubinsky**, *chief learning officer, Ready Learner One LLC*

"Diana speaks with a profoundly genuine and insightful voice in *Copyrighteous*! Her fundamental passion for the ethics of education come through with each word. *Copyrighteous* will not only shine a light on content that many educators have yet to even consider, but it will also bring readers together into a supportive circle of trust. Her focus on trust and collaboration with our peers is key to all of us in education as we continue to grow, because '. . . doing the right thing is usually harder.'"

—**Marcus Painter**, *coordinator of digital learning*

"*Copyrighteous* is not a dry, boring book about copyright. Although it is critical that educators are aware of the legal implications of using and reusing others' work, this book is not about following the rules of copyright to limit a teacher in the classroom. It's about following the rules of copyright to open doors for students, empower teachers, and create a culture of sharing."

—**Michele Eaton**, *director of virtual and blended learning at the M.S.D. of Wayne Township*

"*Copyrighteous* empowers teachers to think outside the box in terms of creativity, while thoughtfully remaining inside the lines of copyright. Educators who read Copyrighteous will be equipped to design, find, and deliver high quality materials for their classrooms."

—**Chris Young**, *strategic learning coordinator, Southern Hancock Schools*

"*Copyrighteous* is such a fitting title for this book! It's catchy and it's meaningful. It not only communicates that it is functionally about copyrights, but artistically it communicates something more. The word righteous can be interpreted as a double entendre, like, 'righteous!' exclaimed in a raspy surfer dude's voice (think Patrick Swayze's character, Bodhi, in the movie Point Break) or righteous, as in religiously considered pure. The message in this book is both fun and fundamental, helpful, and 'hella cool' for educators and students alike. Thank you Diana Gill for producing such a righteous work."

—**Dee Lanier**, *sociologist, educational technologist, and equity enthusiast*

A CATALYST FOR CREATIVITY IN THE CLASSROOM.

COPY RIGHT EOUS

Diana R. Gill

COPYRIGHTEOUS

© 2019 by Diana Gill

This book is available at special discounts when purchased in quantity for use as premiums, promotions, fundraisers, or for educational use. For inquiries and details, contact the publisher at books@dave-burgessconsulting.com.

Published by Dave Burgess Consulting, Inc.
San Diego, CA
http://daveburgessconsulting.com

Editing, Interior, and Cover Design by My Writers' Connection

Library of Congress Control Number: 2019949542
Paperback ISBN: 978-1-949595-78-9
Ebook ISBN: 978-1-949595-79-6

First Printing: October 2019

CONTENTS

DISCLAIMER

I am not a lawyer. I am an educator. I've always known that I wanted to be an educator, and even on the hardest of days, I feel incredibly lucky to love what I do. Somewhere along my journey as an educator, I found myself caring very deeply about the lack of support I felt educators had in relation to applying copyright *and* seeing themselves as creators. Maybe it is because I fought really hard to see myself as a creator in my own classroom. I didn't see myself as a creator until I decided I needed to break the rules to do what was right by my students, which is what led me to understanding how powerful following the rules of copyright could be in my creative process. It's a weird sort of contradiction.

This book is an effort to help educators create in a respectful manner while also bringing respect for the profession as one of creativity. This book is my best interpretation of copyright law, but it is not a substitute for it. My ultimate mission is to make this topic more approachable and bring awareness. However, I hope that after reading *#Copyrighteous*, you wil feel empowered to create a classroom environment that is truly YOU for YOUR students.

DEDICATION

For McKenna and Ryker.
Dream big, my beautiful babies.

FOREWORD

When it comes to copyright law, educators often see it as "one more thing." It is too easy to disregard best practices, and in many situations the odds favor having no consequences to violations of copyright law. But is this modeling behavior for our students that we want them to emulate? In my own journey to better educate teachers and students about copyright, I was introduced to Diana Gill. Diana's approach to copyright best practices comes from a place of teaching and modeling ethical behaviors rather than a fear-based approach about potential lawsuits, damages, and punitive actions.

While not a legal treatise on copyright law, Diana's best practices apply the legal framework found in US copyright law to common scenarios found in educational environments. As an attorney, I have found Diana's approach to be thorough and follow the spirit of the law. As an educator, her methods are helpful and practical. Without hesitation, Diana has my endorsement on both counts.

—**Chad Heck, JD, MLS**

THE CLASS IN A BOX

About nine years ago, I had three years of teaching experience and was starting in a new school. When my department chair gave me the curriculum for my courses—basically a binder for each course, described as a "class in a box"—the look in her eye suggested she was handing me a precious gift, the secrets of the universe. It quickly became clear, however, that this "gift" of a class in a box wasn't really a gift, but instead a pair of handcuffs prohibiting my movement as a professional.

One "class in a box" I taught was a senior-level research-heavy course, complete with a mile-long list of procedures and rules crafted simply to "avoid cheating." In reality, the rules, procedures, and near obsession with everyone doing *everything* the *exact same way* was completely crushing what I hoped my classroom environment to be and what I hoped to build in my students.

I wasn't happy. My students weren't happy. I knew I had to change something. And I did. Through these experiences, I began to find my true voice as a teacher. I was biased toward action and finding a solution. Creating my own materials and rewriting these courses was my reaction to these situations. I was done with "class in a box" and canned curriculum; I was more than willing to "break the rules" of traditional education. Building engaging content and changing the learning experience for my students was my number one priority.

Some of the materials I created were good, but in total transparency, I didn't worry about copyright. I was an English teacher who taught students to cite properly, and I supported information literacy skills, but I didn't hold myself to those same standards. The "beg, borrow, steal" mentality had already been integrated into my practices. I had compartmentalized creating for my classroom as separate from the creating I was asking my students to do. In a subconscious way, I was being disloyal to my students and myself in engaging in a process that wasn't always the most responsible to design the best possible materials for my students.

But eventually, as I found my own voice as a teacher, another layer became clear: I also had to ensure I honored the voices who came before me. Over time, I learned how important it is not only to be creative and do what's best for my students but also to recognize those whose work I was using in the process.

Copyrighteous highlights this power of finding your creative voice as a teacher—including locating, using, and building on others' ideas and resources—while honoring the rules of copyright as part of this process. This book is about asking, sharing, and citing instead of begging, borrowing, and stealing. Ultimately it's about following the rules of copyright to break the rules of education.

Additionally, I wrote *Copyrighteous* to empower teachers and students to find their creative voices and share what they create through an understanding of copyright and protection of intellectual property. Along with narrative stories, I've also given practical strategies to support teachers as they make related shifts in the classroom. But *Copyrighteous* is not just for teachers. Superintendents, building leaders, teachers, and students can all contribute to this culture of sharing when they learn that copyright really can be a catalyst for creativity.

PART ONE:
RECORD

=

Your Teacher LP

CHAPTER 1
Authentic Teacher Voice

The first step toward finding your authentic teacher voice is through building relationships with your students. In her 2013 Ted Talk, Rita Pierson states, "Kids don't learn from people they don't like," speaking largely to the mantra of educators everywhere: relationships are what matter. While I find Pierson's statement to be profound and incredibly honest, I am inspired to take her train of thought one step further and declare, "Students don't learn from people they don't know." The foundation of what educators do lies entirely in the relationships they build with each other, their students, and with parents. Remembering this is important when we curate and design content for our students to learn. No matter the mode of learning, relationships matter.

Think about the online class you took, requiring you to complete a discussion board every week. What conclusions did you draw when the instructor didn't respond to your comments or interact with the class in any way? By contrast, think about those vulnerable moments when you did something silly and your class forgave you for it—but teased you anyway. Or how someone in your class could tell you what sweater you wore on Thursday two weeks ago. Students notice everything. For example, have you ever had a student write, "I'm so sorry you have to read this!" in the middle of an essay—both to say "hi" and to see if you are paying attention? They notice whether you are attentive or not. In return, you must also pay attention—to who you are and who your students are. And not just in these peripheral moments. Your attention should carry over into everything you do. What you might consider to be peripheral to the curriculum is actually the core of all you do.

Getting to know your students and letting them get to know you is all part of building relationships with them. One of my senior students once told me the first week of my class felt like a "getting to know you" exercise. And yes, it was—by design! Perhaps I overdid it, but I knew if I was going to work with my students to get them to write ten-page research papers, we had to know each other and trust each other. They had to trust I was going to follow through on their expectations, and I had to trust our relationship would make them feel comfortable enough to learn.

On the first day of school one year, I ditched outlining student expectations and had students share their expectations of me instead. I gave students stacks of sticky notes and asked them to write down the things they expected of me as a teacher. I prompted them to think about what they expected me to do, what things they needed me to do for them to be successful, and what they needed me to avoid. I told the students the notes should be anonymous and asked them to put the notes on the whiteboard as they walked out of the room. Another year, students wrote the same points on a piece of paper—before I asked them to turn it into a paper airplane and let it fly across the room! Giving trust to the students before they "earned it" was central to showing them that I am human, and we have a shared role in what happens in the classroom.

My daughter, McKenna, is now a kindergarten student, so I get to experience school as a new "school mom." I now also see how much teachers invest in their students from a different perspective. Adjusting to school as a new kindergartener is a huge undertaking, and my daughter experienced some tummy issues as a result. As we tried to figure out the cause, we decided to eliminate dairy. (She had been taking full advantage of the chocolate milk available at lunch!) When her teacher, Mrs. Wilson, became aware of the tummy issue, and we spoke about avoiding milk at lunch, she personally made sure McKenna did not take a milk with her school lunch (even though the cafeteria staff had very strong opinions about calcium intake!). Mrs. Wilson helped her smuggle in a water bottle so she had something to drink with her lunch. On another occasion, my daughter left her lunch at home. I was out of town, and her dad was not able to leave work to take the lunch to school. Mrs. Wilson noticed the only options for lunch (pizza and pizza) were heavily dairy. She was concerned and contacted the principal, who then contacted me with a plan. They were ready to create a different lunch for my daughter to accommodate for the forgotten lunch and her tummy issues.

My point isn't about my daughter not eating dairy; it's about teachers building relationships with their students. The point is how well teachers know their students and how well they care for them—to the point of being willing to "break the rules" (smuggling in a water bottle) for the best interest of a student. Later, feeling guilty about the forgotten lunch, I emailed the teacher to tell her how grateful I was and how happy I was to have her as part of my village. As a parent, I feel thankful my daughter has amazing people at school looking out for her—her math skills, reading skills, and her internal organs.

These relationships are exactly why I—as a teacher—will always choose creativity over a "canned" curriculum. Creativity allows me to tailor curriculum based on my relationships with my students, giving me an authentic voice in the classroom. Although a sweet spot can be found between mandating a scripted curriculum and providing enough resources for teachers, educators must be sure the way they implement resources or their approach to implementing curriculum allows for teacher flexibility. In any classroom—brick and mortar, virtual, or blended—relationships are central to learning. If administrators do not give teachers an opportunity to create, remix, curate, and build a set of resources reflecting who they are, who their students are, and their specific learning environment, they are forgetting that relationships matter. Educators must consider relationships as part of all they do. Relationships are central to the instructional materials teachers use and the activities guiding learning in schools.

SINGING LOUDLY WHILE STAYING IN TUNE

Educators need the same opportunities for voice and choice that they offer to their students. Teachers can design content because they are in the classrooms interacting with students. They are the only ones who can immediately respond to their students' needs and interests—the only ones who can design with their class's specific personality in mind. If you ignore this, you are ignoring the power of the teacher. Educators might not be instructional designers by name, but we have an opportunity to take advantage of the skills we have built and believe we are designers even before it is manifested fully.

When I advocate for teacher voice, encouraging teachers to design content rooted in relationship with students, I am speaking of designing activities to implement and teach curriculum. I am not suggesting they are designing *curriculum*. One of my biggest beefs in educational practices is the tendency to use language inaccurately. Likely you can identify at least one buzzword that is quick to get under your skin. Educators often throw around these buzzwords but don't use them correctly, further perpetuating misunderstandings. In an effort to avoid this situation, I want to clarify what I mean when I use *curriculum*.

I imagine someone who is skeptical about teachers being given the freedom to dictate how they implement their curriculum on a daily basis is visualizing the "wild west" of education—everyone shooting from the hip. This criticism might be based on many things, and the concerns might be valid. There are situations in which we need to come together to be sure that a common curriculum is driving our collective efforts. In other situations, the need to control what is happening could be just that—control, or even professional jealousy.

CURRICULUM GUIDES THE PATH YOU TAKE, BUT YOU GET TO DECIDE WHAT TO WEAR, EAT, AND DO ALONG THE PATH.

Curriculum should be built and reflected on as a team and implemented with effectiveness. The activities, resources, and instructional materials teachers each use might differ, but the curriculum itself should not. The creative freedoms I speak to are the decisions about how to address curriculum—not what the curriculum consists of.

Curriculum is the structure of the building—the wood, bricks, and mortar. You work with your team to make decisions about curriculum, and everyone agrees to build a specific structure with their students. Teacher professionalism, freedom, and creativity comes in the nuanced ways each teacher shows his or her students how to lay the bricks and apply the mortar. Teachers decide what tools to use with students to achieve a sound structure. Teachers decide what finishes to use and what overall ambiance the structure will radiate. Curriculum cannot be scripted.

When I speak of teachers designing educational resources rooted in relationship with their students, I am not suggesting they abandon the agreed-on curriculum and forge through a completely isolated path. Curriculum guides the path you take, but you get to decide what to wear, eat, and do along the path.

As you're making those decisions along the path, keep in mind that students can be honest—brutally honest. If they don't like something, they will let you know. If they think something you are asking them to do is too hard or too fast, they will tell you. At least my kiddos always did. Personally, I enjoyed this. I think their willingness to be so open came from my creating a culture allowing them to feel comfortable doing so. Or perhaps I am giving myself too much credit and they would have either way, but I can say that I reflected on and responded to their feedback. Though at times constructive criticism can be hard to swallow, I loved learning from it. In each role I've had as an educator, I have felt compelled to be transparent about what happens behind the scenes. In the classroom, this manifested in my sharing the process of planning with my students—when it made sense to. For example, when students complained openly about something we were doing, I asked them straight up, "Do you know who made this activity?" I'll admit there were moments when I took those complaints personally. I wanted them to know they were openly hating on something I made or remixed. (For the record, I'm fine with criticism—just not complaining without offering solutions.) If there was a reason to revisit an activity, we did.

We also had similar conversations about the novels we read. When a student complained about a book we were reading, I offered support and reassurance. If I heard incessant complaints, I asked the class, "Do you think I get to choose the books?" They answered, "Yes!" In this situation, the books we read were the "path" given to me, but I got to choose the resources and activities I used in class to teach skills. My students' honesty allowed me to see more from their perspective. I could then reflect on their input and adjust as needed.

LYRICS ARE EVERYTHING

Beg, borrow, and steal has been a mantra in education. You've definitely heard it before and, like most educators, you've probably *said* it a time or two in your career (I've said it dozens of times!). This phrase celebrates searching for, collecting, and using the best ideas educators can get their hands on for their students. For some, *beg, borrow, and steal* has become a maxim to live by. I'm not sure where this phrase originated, but I'm confident it was created with good intentions. Teachers want to cultivate environments in which students can engage in learning, be challenged, and create new content. Why wouldn't people applaud going to great lengths to accomplish this? In fact, the world expects educators to do this.

But take a second look at this phrase. The word *beg* implies educators have to make some sort of grand appeal to use something in their class-rooms. The word *borrow* is kinder, yet it suggests teachers eventually have to return what they use. Why can't they keep it? And *steal?* Yikes! Why are educators stealing? Would they encourage their students to steal an idea or resource? Hopefully not.

Why haven't educators expanded their verbiage beyond the use of this phrase? They have elevated their educational practices in so many ways; they need to think about the message this educational cliché sends to oth-ers. The words they choose leave a mark. Consider the mark these words leave on those new to education, those in field work or doing their student teaching, or the brand-new educators walking into their first classroom. Is *beg, borrow, and steal* the message you want to pass on to them?

Educators must be better. They must revise this phrase to fit a world in which teachers have the opportunity to connect and explore constantly. Instead of begging, educators should feel comfortable *asking* colleagues for permission to use their materials. Rather than borrowing ideas, teach-ers should readily *share* their content with others seeking to give the best to their students. And instead of stealing, educators should always prop-erly *cite* materials to acknowledge their originator. *Asking, sharing,* and *cit-ing* ensures that all educators not only find the very best resources for their students, but that they can do so in a way they feel good about.

As educators you must be intentional about the words you choose, because they define your craft. You aren't beggars, borrowers, and steal-ers. You are designers and creators, and you are instructors who are part of a larger community. The words you use impact the culture of your schools, in both the short term and the long term. When you use a buzzword or apply an educational term incorrectly, you are making it more difficult for the real message to spread. When you use *beg, borrow,* and *steal,* you give yourself—and others—permission to make a potentially unsound choice. For example, when you use the word "steal" to describe the process of planning, you aren't considering the light you cast on the work you do. No educator would list "thief" as a job role or responsibility. In reality, when educators casually use "steal," they are probably describing something closer to *inspired by* or *remixed from.*

CHAPTER 2
Breaking the Rules

This spring, my four-year-old son, Ryker, played t-ball for the first time at our local YMCA. He had already been through a couple of soccer seasons with his fair share of tears, but at his first t-ball practice, he was very excited! He had been practicing the "rules" of fielding and hitting. During the practice, Ryker's coach directed him to stand on the pitcher's mound when it was his turn on the field. He obediently stood in his spot and waited for the hits to come his direction. Not surprisingly, the attentions of these three- and four-year-olds tended to wander, and soon, two additional teammates were standing on the pitcher's mound with Ryker. His "uh-oh" look quickly took over his face, and after making eye contact with me, he ran off the field as tears started to build.

Ryker feels very strongly about doing the right thing. I knew immediately he was upset because he felt others were not following the rules. I tried to explain to him that his job was to listen to his coach and play the position he was assigned; he couldn't get upset about the actions of others. We talked later about this being the first practice and everyone was learning the rules of the game, and we talked about the need to be patient with others as they find their place on the field.

As Ryker experienced, when people choose to ignore the rules, their actions will impact other people. Although this impact can be negative at times, I had an epiphany when I realized I could positively impact my classroom by breaking the rules of education.

HITTING THE HIGH NOTES (RULE BREAKING 101)

My introduction to breaking the rules came when my department chair gave me the "classes in a box" and asked me to "stay on the same page" and teach certain topics (*i.e.*, essentially worksheets) on certain days. Her rationale was that the original course designer had a ton of experience and the department had been doing it *just like this* for quite some time. Additionally, they wanted to ensure we were all on the same page as a possible reaction to questions from parents. Essentially, she wanted to avoid the type of phone calls that inquired why one teacher was making instructional choices or asking students to accomplish a task that another teacher was not.

As I mentioned earlier, as I set out to be a good employee, doing what I was asked, I quickly decided these "classes in a box" stifled me as a teacher and cultivated a climate of compliance for my students. For example, the grammar worksheets I was asked to cover weren't creating the engaging environment I had envisioned.

After sticking to the script for a semester, I asked my department chair for permission to make a few changes in one of these scripted courses. I promised I would cover the material given but suggested I could do it in a different way and perhaps add additional content and activities. I was persuasive, and she gave me permission; however, on the first day of the new semester, I was called in for questioning. After taking my students to a lab to set up blogs, my department chair accused me of not covering the material. Immediately, I knew I had a decision to make: I would either have to stick to the script or accept that I would have to defend every single decision I made for my classroom.

During this season, when I had to defend all my decisions, I was also teaching the senior-level heavy-research class I mentioned earlier. Not only did this class come with a scripted curriculum, but it also came with a very specific set of classroom rules we were to follow. These students, many of whom were eighteen, were each given a folder to organize all of their research materials and were asked to keep all class materials in the classroom. If the folders left the room, I was to deduct points. Additionally, students were not allowed to access research materials after the research part of the process was over. (Forget honoring growth and reflection!) At the time, we were working with the computer lab model, and the educator in charge of lab supervision was responsible for catching violations if I did not (and I never did, because I was more concerned with teaching my students than counting folders!).

Students were allowed to completely design their own paper topics, which was not part of the original plan given to me, and one student came to class very excited about his topic. Earlier in the day, a discussion in his history class had sparked something he wanted to research and include in his paper for my class. He walked into the lab with some notes, sat down at his computer, and started to get to work. He had collected a ton of ideas from his history teacher about how to improve the concept of his paper, and he was excited!

Isn't this exactly what educators want? He was a making cross-curricular connections, taking complete ownership of his writing, and getting truly pumped about creating something new—until the lab supervisor, designated rule enforcer of the space, walked over to the student, took his notes away, accused him of cheating, and threw his notes in the garbage!

Unfortunately, I was absent when this happened and was told about it upon my return. In the moment I learned about it, a switch inside me flipped forever. This final straw broke the proverbial camel's back. I decided I was okay with "breaking the rules" and getting into "trouble" every single day if it meant this situation never happened again.

What do I mean by "breaking the rules" of education? Breaking the rules is constantly reevaluating what works with your students, what is relevant to them, and what is responsive to their needs and personalities. By breaking the rules, you are continually ensuring your students are receiving the best possible educational experiences.

TEACHERS WILLING TO "BREAK THE RULES" AREN'T CHANGING FOR THE SAKE OF CHANGE; RATHER, THEY ARE MOVING TOWARD THEIR RESPONSIBILITY TO TEACH AUTHENTICALLY.

· · · · · · · · · · ·

I was once criticized by a superior who said she didn't understand why I felt the need to revolutionize everything I taught every year. To me, teaching the same thing and using the same resources every year without reflection defines maintaining the status quo. Textbooks become outdated. Resources and curriculum must be allowed to live, breathe, grow, and change. Teachers willing to "break the rules" aren't changing for the sake of change; rather, they are moving toward their responsibility to teach authentically. Breaking the rules isn't a "one and done." It's a teaching lifestyle.

Certainly, I'm not suggesting we throw the baby out with the bathwater every year and completely start over. Some resources work from year to year. Some require minor tweaks. Some should be abandoned when we learn more and can do even better. Constantly reevaluating and knowing how you can adjust your resources supports you in this process.

Breaking the rules of education is also anything that disrupts your definition of "traditional classroom." You know the one: students seated in rows of desks, silently consuming content as the teacher—standing at the front of the room and the only one speaking—holds the students captive, hoping as much content as possible will stick. Thankfully, as so many educators embrace the power of connected learning, this is a far cry from what brick-and-mortar schools look like now. Yet, while teachers aren't "walking uphill both ways" to their one-room schoolhouses, educators still need to make a lot of shifts to get to a place where they honor authentic learning and skill building over consumption of content only. Using flexible materials is one shift educators can make to honor what they know to be true: students should be empowered in the classroom and should be central to the decisions made about a learning environment.

Breaking the rules of education is constantly re-evaluating, shifting, and redesigning what you do in your classroom. Even the very best lessons won't work forever. You should be in a constant state of reflection. If you are honestly reflecting on all parts of what you do, specifically focusing on the instructional materials and learning experiences you are creating for your students, you will also continually improve as an educator.

I was—and still am—willing to break the rules. But as Michael Port writes in his book, *Steal the Show*, breaking the rules and finding your voice isn't about rebellion; it is about creating something new. I was not seeking to rebel against the rules of a scripted curriculum, but I had to do what I absolutely knew was right to do for my students—no matter what. I had to do more than follow a script. I began to create my own lessons, and I turned to digital materials and technology tools for help. Finding my teacher voice in this way enabled me to create something new and better.

And I realize the contradiction here: I am working to spread the message of following the rules of copyright while encouraging educators to break the rules still existing in many spaces of traditional education. So what gives? What path do I follow to know when it is okay to break the rules? It's simple: I break the rules when it's the right thing to do for students—and no one gets hurt.

CHARACTERISTICS OF A "RULE-BREAKING" CLASSROOM

While the specific details will likely vary from classroom to classroom, generally the following characteristics will be found in classrooms where educators are breaking the rules of traditional education:

BREAKING THE RULES OF EDUCATION IS CONSTANTLY RE-EVALUATING, SHIFTING, AND REDESIGNING WHAT YOU DO IN YOUR CLASSROOM.

Educators design nontraditional experiences for students. Just as teachers want to be honored as professionals through using their voice and personality, educators should ensure that they are also honoring their students as creators. Teachers must put students at the center of the learning process. For example, are you giving your students the opportunity to engage in learning as content producers? Are you asking them to solve real problems? Are you giving them an opportunity to make their own decisions about pace, content, delivery, and product creation? Are you truly letting them take ownership of their learning?

Teachers function as the "lead learner and explorer" instead of the owner of knowledge. Because teachers and students have constant access to unlimited information, no one person can be an expert on anything. Educators must stop thinking of themselves as experts of content. Instead, they must shift their self-view, seeing themselves as experts in instruction and pedagogy—not simply content. When you don't know the answer to something, find out along with your students. Develop powerful lines of inquiry instead of simply sharing answers to questions. Even better, teach your students to ask questions themselves.

Physical classroom space is used creatively for learning. A nontraditional classroom is physically designed to complement learning—not manage behavior. Does your space allow for flexibility, thoughtful grouping, and collaboration? You've probably heard a lot about flexible seating and, if you've done your research, you know expensive equipment is available. But just as technology tools won't solely transform teaching and learning, fancy furniture won't either. The good news is that you can be creative with the furniture and space you already have. Simply shift your intentions (and maybe a few tables and chairs also!). Ditch the seating charts and rows used to keep students on task (another "I've done it" confession here!). Make your space supportive of the type of learning and teaching you want to see in your classroom. Your physical space can be just as flexible as your teaching methods and materials.

Educators leverage new and ever-changing technology. Technology can't replace teachers, but it can certainly support good teaching. A "rule-breaking" classroom allows new technology to inspire innovative ways to learn and create. Technology can help students show their learning by creating while fostering information and media literacy. This topic alone could be an entire book—and already is the topic of countless books! Bottom line, if you aren't currently using technology in your classroom, your students are missing out. You can be a good teacher without technology, but you have a moral obligation to use the tools available to you to foster the skills your students deserve—and need—to be successful.

Although we might assume a traditional classroom is devoid of technology, the presence or absence of technology itself isn't necessarily indicative of innovative learning. But I would be skipping over a huge point if I didn't mention how technology plays a crucial role in outlining what a traditional classroom is and is not. Differentiation, personalized learning, and finding time to work more closely with students in a mentoring role would be incredibly difficult without the implementation of blended learning executed with technology.

Teachers seek to break out of the four walls of their classroom. Using technology such as a simple Google Hangout video call or Skype call, you can take your students literally anywhere in the world to meet anyone—encouraging cross-curricular teaching on an entirely different plane. The only hurdle you have is to reach out and ask! You can use virtual tours to take your students on field trips previously inconceivable, or to connect your students with other learners around the globe. Physically, you and your students might meet within the same four walls every day, but in reality, you're not required to stay there.

Educators and students focus on building skills instead of consuming content. A nontraditional classroom prioritizes skill building—academic standards and soft skills—over memorizing and teaching content. Instead of churning out identical products when students graduate, you encourage the four C's: critical thinking, collaboration, creativity, and communication. If you are keeping these things at the center of what you do when you design learning activities, you are creating activities that allow your students to learn actively.

The idea of "getting through the material" is discarded. I wish I had realized this sooner in my career! In a nontraditional classroom, teachers recognize it is more important to dive deep into skills and analysis than it is to rattle off content on a prescriptive timeline. Valuing skills over content is most of the battle. Additionally, you must ask yourself whether hitting every skill on the list is more important than mastering skills before moving on too quickly.

Both teachers and students are allowed to take risks. Risk-taking has become a buzzword in education. While I've already shared that I can become sick of buzzwords, this is one we can't brush off. It became a "buzz" word for a reason, right? Just as administrators should encourage teachers to take risks to be creative, teachers must do the same for students. When educators have a growth mindset, they create a safe space for teachers and students to fail, making risk-taking much less...risky. How's that for a "buzzwordy" sentence?! Risk-taking and the opportunity to fail in a safe space give teachers—and students—room to reflect and time to plan for and take action toward improvement.

Student needs inform instruction. Rather than allowing content to drive the classroom, a "rule-breaking" classroom allows student needs to inform teaching and learning. When you shift to a student-centered classroom and constantly make decisions through the lens of student learning objectives, you start with student needs and build from there. In a more traditional classroom, student needs are often an afterthought.

RISK-TAKING: A WALK IN THE GUTTER

One professor I especially enjoyed as an education major undergrad was a fairly "ancient" man (his words) who had collected many stories throughout his teaching experience. Sometimes after finishing the basics of a topic in class, he would give us this dark look and say, "Now let's get into the gutter. Let's really talk about the truth of this—what it looks like in the real world." When I have the opportunity to speak to preservice teachers, I try to channel this professor. After sharing my memories of him, I tell the teachers I want to try to bust through the myths and buzzwords of education—specifically within the scope of educational technology. I tell them I want to get into the "gutter."

As I tell them, so much of what you do in your classroom can be dictated by the school you are working in. I might never have been ready to take the risk to step out of the classroom and become a full-time technology coach if my school hadn't asked me to help with technology leadership work. I may not have had the confidence to pursue those leadership roles if I hadn't worked in a school using online snow days earlier than the rest of our area of the state. I have worked in a school with a lot of access to technology, and in a school with very little access to technology.

By contrast, sometimes you must personally carve out space for these opportunities. When I was in a non–1:1 classroom and desperately wanted students to engage using technology tools, we busted out cell phones—totally against school board policy! (Don't worry, my principal gave us the blessing.)

- If you work in a district that supports risk-taking, take advantage of that.
- If you work in a district that doesn't support risk-taking, do it anyway.

I say this over and over again to preservice educators. While this is an ask-for-forgiveness approach that my current district-level administrator self might guffaw at, my true teacher soul screams, "Go for it!"

On the flip side, if you find yourself in an environment where these types of experiences are not naturally available, you have to make them for yourself. If you truly are making decisions for the benefit of students, who could argue with you? And if you truly are making decisions based on what is best for students and someone still chooses to argue with you, who cares? You certainly shouldn't. But I ask of you, don't get yourself fired. We have to keep our jobs to teach children, right?! However, if there is space to challenge someone's thinking, go for it. This is why teachers exist: to make people think! Personally, I thrive when I'm surrounded by people who challenge my thinking.

IF YOU WORK IN A DISTRICT THAT SUPPORTS RISK-TAKING, TAKE ADVANTAGE OF THAT. IF YOU WORK IN A DISTRICT THAT DOESN'T SUPPORT RISK-TAKING, DO IT ANYWAY.

· · · · · · · · · · ·

And herein lies the contradiction: aren't I sharing this book to ask you to follow the rules of copyright? Yes! Because sometimes following the rules is appropriate and best. But you have to know when it is in your best interest—and the best interest of your students—to fall in line and when it makes sense to push against the rules. Ironically, sometimes one is necessary to do the other.

SINGING A RIFF

One of the nonfiction books I was required to read with my ninth-grade students was *Hiroshima* by John Hersey. Personally, I loved the book, but the first time I read it with students, I found they really struggled. We worked through the tougher text together, and we had great conversations about historical events, wrote argumentative essays on related topics, and discussed the lives of real people and the real consequences of decisions made during this time of war. Their experience reading this nonfiction text was much different from their response to reading other texts in class.

The next year, I knew I had to pull out all the stops to support my students. I worked with other teachers to create a video to provide helpful background information. We gave the book as much historical context as possible. We listened to speeches from presidents. We made character charts and posted them all over the room. We held after-school book clubs. We met in small groups during student resource time so those struggling to get through the independent reading could move through it together. We ordered sushi and learned about Japanese culture. Wait. Sushi? When my supervisor discovered we ordered sushi, I was accused of bribing my students to read their book. (Yes, bribe was the word actually used.) In the moment, I felt crushed. Eventually I learned I didn't have to do all those things, and I gradually adjusted a lot of what I did for this book. But, at the time, I felt I had accomplished something significant with my students to get them engaged. I was excited by the relationships we were forging through rich debates about presidential decisions and experiencing culture through food. My response to my supervisor's accusation was, "I'm not bribing them." (Nice one, Diana!) After six years to think about it, I should have said something like, "I am not going to apologize for working as hard as I can to create an engaging and enriching learning experience for my students, thank you very much."

This story perfectly exemplifies the difference between traditional teaching and teaching in a skills-focused environment. Who really cares what book you choose to teach as long as your students are learning essential skills? Many of the skills our students need in relation to language arts have little to do with knowing the plot of every book in the literary canon—and I am not against the canon, mind you (#HarperLeeForever). When I saw that a certain text I was giving to reluctant readers was only deepening their reluctance, I wanted to address that and work to inspire a love of reading.

Another experience occurred during adoption year, when we had a lot of conversations about which required readings and novels we wanted the school board to approve. I'll never forget the conversation around *Ready Player One*. When this book was released, I gave it to anyone I thought might cling to it. If a student had a good sense of humor, an appreciation for anything vintage, talked about Minecraft, or mentioned being tired from staying up too late, I practically sprinted to get a copy of the book into their hands. Every single person I gave this book to—student and adult—fell in love with it. So of course, I suggested we adopt it as an official ninth-grade reading. But it was turned down—not enough "literary merit."

Educators must take advantage of the opportunity to respond to the performance trends they see in students. By responding, you can collectively use your powers of curating, remixing, and creating your own high-quality instructional content to help your students grow. If you are only creating your own content for your classrooms with the goal of simply being different, you are not leveraging all of the possibilities risk-taking can give you, and I mostly make this point in response to the criticisms I personally received.

To illustrate this idea, think about a standard or skill you love to teach. You spend hours perfecting your lessons and resources to get students excited about the skill, and you watch them grow. Responding to feedback and to keep things relevant, each year you make subtle changes to your lesson related to the skill. This is a highlight for you because you see your students totally "get it." In a grade-level meeting, another teacher shares that her students are struggling with the same standard or skill you are absolutely killing and asks what others are using to help students master the learning objective. You take the opportunity to help, and now, something you made, found, or created is impacting another classroom in a significant way. This is far different from everyone having to do the same thing on the same day in the same way.

Keep in mind, however, that responding to all challenges by throwing buzzwords around doesn't let you off the hook. Saying, "I'm a risk-taker!" and, "It's the best thing for the students!" loses all meaning when you use them as excuses. Although you definitely should be taking risks and making decisions based on what is best for your students, discovering what is best for them may sometimes mean taking a hard look at the data and recognizing that you might need to make a change or two. Sometimes what is best for kids is being willing to recognize your own weaknesses as an instructor and taking advantage of any opportunity to grow.

Educators must hold themselves and each other accountable. An educational culture that sees its teachers as creators can have honest conversations about how instructional practices can impact instruction. Letting data inform your instructional decisions, when coupled with creative freedom, can be completely transformational.

CHAPTER 3 ▷
Breaking the Rules
through Design

My "class in a box" experience, among others, made me passionate about breaking the rules and designing educational resources in order to provide the best materials for my students. Ultimately, these experiences also brought me to digital resources and are central to many of my beliefs about education, so I share my story regularly. In fact, I have brazenly said that I don't want to work in an environment in which teacher freedom is not respected. But I needed to be reminded that freedom leaves the door open for others as well—even to make a different decision from one I might prefer.

One morning, I shared my story with a group of teachers as part of a personal learning community (PLC), and afterward, one of the building leaders reflected with me on the conversation we had with his staff. He is an incredibly thoughtful leader, and I was eager to hear his feedback. He reminded me that not everyone is looking to create and curate instructional materials; some of his teachers prefer a scripted curriculum they can follow. Although this shouldn't have surprised me, it did.

How can teachers be creative when they don't want to design from scratch? Thankfully, a lot of high-quality content and courses are available; however, as you evaluate them and consider their use in your classroom, you ultimately come across questions you would ask differently, projects you would modify, or phrases you would add to introduce a concept to your students. No canned program perfectly mirrors what you want for your classroom. Nothing a school can purchase for you will be you. No prepackaged curriculum will automatically respond to your students' interests, class culture, or passion projects. From year to year, the needs of your classroom change, and the next adoption cycle—even if you can wait for it—may not meet those needs. But a thoughtful curation process and a collection of resources quite possibly can.

Digital resources allowing for modifications and remixing is a step toward meeting the unique needs of a class without requiring a teacher to create from scratch. When you evaluate purchased resources or ones found online, you should first look for permission to modify, adapt, or remix. Although this is directly linked to responsible use and an understanding of copyright, the ultimate purpose is to be compelling, not compliant. Your why should be to modify resources to create a final product that is best for your students—not to be a rule follower.

THE ULTIMATE PURPOSE IS TO BE COMPELLING, NOT COMPLIANT.

· · · · · · · · · · ·

Curating and creating instructional materials is harder than using scripted curriculum; it requires more time and effort. Schools and educators also must clearly communicate their intent when making decisions about which resources are to be provided for teachers. For example, allowing teachers to curate and create doesn't mean schools don't provide resources, and it doesn't mean that we forgo resource adoption altogether. Instead, moving toward more teacher creativity helps schools shift the process of planning and adoption. If educators find value in teacher-curated and created materials and find risk-taking a powerful approach to teaching and learning, then they have to change the process from start to finish. What would the textbook adoption process look like if we could approach it from the frame of creating and curating, either instead of or alongside adoption? Many schools are choosing to forego traditional textbooks and are thoughtfully allocating resources in a different way. What would your daily schedule look like if your school made it a priority to provide you the support and time to curate and create? What would education look like if this were done intentionally with our teachers for our students?

Educators can start to adjust what their process looks like, but they can't have a conversation about remixing materials and honoring copyright without digging into the definition of pedagogy. I see people make this mistake when schools go "paperless." Personally, I push against this term because many interpret this as "because we are 1:1 with technology, we don't need an adoption process at all." Although that might be true, the message sent to teachers is that they are losing support. Going "paperless" shouldn't be the goal. Instead, providing resources in a way other than textbook adoption—either digital or print—can be done thoughtfully, and, ultimately, it can be incredibly powerful, but schools still must provide resources and time to this end. Simply "not adopting" isn't enough. If a school staff works together and finds that curating and creating is a preferred method to textbook adoption, they have to be sure that there are supports in place for teachers.

Educators also should not make this decision (curating vs. textbook adoption) focused on only cost savings. Curating and creating require an investment of time and money. And I repeat: Creating and curating do take time. I don't want to pretend that it doesn't take hard work. Shifting to this process will be a large time investment, but the payoff is huge. Investing in the curation and creation of the materials you use with your students is an investment in more than just the materials themselves; it is an investment in the relationships you have with your students—the most critical aspect of any educator's role.

INVESTING IN THE CURATION AND CREATION OF THE MATERIALS YOU USE WITH YOUR STUDENTS IS AN INVESTMENT IN MORE THAN JUST THE MATERIALS THEMSELVES.

. . . .

How does all of this connect to copyright? Current technology means that educators don't have to create materials from scratch for them to be high quality. In the same way you've left behind memorized recipes, moved through cookbooks, and now use eMeals (thank you!) to whip up amazing dishes, technology gives you access to numerous resources for developing high-quality content. Although creating materials from scratch is deeply satisfying, you now have many ways to create learning experiences for your students without taking on one hundred percent of the weight. The saying "two heads are better than one" applies infinitely here; the Internet provides immeasurable brain power to support and challenge you when creating digital content.

With this power comes responsibility, however - specifically, the obligation to create responsibly. I consider this "information literacy" for teachers. In my writing classes, I guided students through the research and writing process. I showed them how to find high-quality information, how to sift through it to choose what would best support their project, and how to use the information in a new way by analyzing it and adding their own arguments and conclusions. Through these steps, students created one new package highlighting their own voices. Creating materials for your students should mimic this process. Focusing on these same steps will support you in curating, remixing, and creating digital content.

IS "TEMPLATE" A DIRTY WORD?

Templates can be a great resource for teachers who want to design but don't want to create entirely from scratch. Some might argue that templates are hurtful, but my experience has shown me that they can actually be quite helpful. A primary responsibility in my current role as an instructional leader is to design professional learning for adults. In 2019, my district began to implement what our state calls Virtual Option for Inclement Weather. This gives schools the flexibility to offer online learning days.

As part of the process to initiate this option, I worked with teachers to design and redesign a number of templates to help us use our learning management system (LMS), provide consistency to students, and design bundles to include what we believed was high-quality virtual instruction and learning.

As someone who believes in supporting teacher creative freedom, I struggled as I worked on these templates. My internal conversation went something like:

We are brick-and-mortar teachers. Online learning asks us to rethink our design, not simply attempt to imitate our face-to-face learning.

Templates will cripple our creativity.

But this is our first time doing this, so we need to provide a level of consistency for parents.

If someone told me to use a template, I might throw it in the garbage.

We have to support everyone and meet them where they are. We have to provide resources.

Our teachers are incredible and will take offense at this.

In the end, I compromised with myself and worked with others to build a starting point—a collection of building blocks or a toolbox. In hindsight, I wish I'd never used the word "template," because I was aware it could send the wrong message. In fact, I found myself avoiding the word "template" at all costs when I worked with teachers to analyze and adjust these resources. One of our secondary teachers suggested we call them something else entirely, and we arrived at "adaptable designs." The items didn't change, but we hoped the different name better communicated what we were hoping to accomplish.

Consider what you expect when you give your students a template. Are you looking for thirty identical products? I hope not. My goal for our online learning lessons is likely what yours is for your students—for them to find a way to infuse personality into the template they start from. The template can be the bones, but you get to add the meat, blood, organs, skin—you get the point!

When teachers design using a template, they need to be empowered to modify and remix it so the result looks, feels, and sounds like *them*—not the template. A template can be a great place to start, of course. You don't have to reinvent the wheel every time you design, but sometimes the wheel can get you where you want to go.

HOW CAN TEACHERS BE CREATIVE/DESIGNERS WHEN THEY'RE GIVEN CANNED CURRICULUM?

Familiar among educators is a strange fear someone will force them to teach in a way they are not comfortable with. The fear manifests loudly at any indication or allusion to this. For example, think about "common assessments." Common assessments can be powerful. Common assessments can open a door to partner with someone else who excels at teaching a skill I might have a weakness with. Unfortunately, the phrase includes the word "common," and when this idea is introduced, you may have several questions quickly pop into your head :

- If another teacher and I are giving the same test, do we have to teach the exact same things and in the exact same way?
- If our test is the same, where does the "sameness" stop?

How can educators design when they're given canned curriculum? First, they must circle back around to pedagogy. All tools can be misused. Common assessments paired with a common daily scripted curriculum isn't the same method as using common assessment data to curate and create better materials to fit the needs of your students. Although some teachers' fears can be attributed to unfair assumptions they make, many of their fears can stem from poor communication, weak vision, and unclear messages. These unclear messages led me to ignore the professional development (PD) at which I was to be given access to my online textbook. And if I'm being really honest, much of my feelings on this could be attributed to my own assumptions. I ignored the content of the meeting because I didn't plan to use an online textbook and because I refused to be locked in. My stubbornness may have made me miss out on some high-quality resources I could have leveraged. As a secondary point, there often is a breakdown of communication coming from all sides of an initiative such as this. Educators must recognize this and know that choosing resources can be very personal, so we have to consider this as we discuss, plan, and execute.

I also faced this fear of being locked in during the last textbook adoption cycle I participated in as a classroom teacher—when a canned curriculum textbook came across my desk. The book was a day-by-day script of what to do, what to say, and what to ask students to do. I had been working so hard to remix and constantly reevaluate the materials I was using to cover skills in my classroom, so the sight of the book sent me into a tailspin. My head was flooded with questions—most of them with negative connotations: *Is this the direction we are going? Am I going to have to follow this? Am I going to have to throw out everything I've been working on?* I hear these same questions from classroom teachers quite frequently, and they are often prompted by something much less direct than a scripted textbook during an adoption cycle. Sometimes these fears come from simple conversations with administrators, or from district initiatives.

Instead of feeling fearful, I could have asked myself how I could use this book to improve my teaching, how these resources might fill some gaps in my current instruction, or what pieces of this material my students could benefit from. But these weren't my thoughts. I just internally freaked out. Looking back, I realize I didn't have to freak out. Ultimately, I could have made the decision—as a professional—to implement the book as a resource in a way appropriate for my classroom. It would have only dictated my day-to-day teaching if I had let it.

I'm reminded of my friend Bill, an incredible teacher I taught with for a few years until he relocated to a different part of the state. Bill is the kind of teacher who, after being observed by an administrator, gets feedback like, "This was one of the very best lessons I've ever observed." Bill and I had shared many discussions about teacher creativity, so when I visited him at his new school the year after he moved, I was shocked to see this same textbook in his classroom. How could Bill—the dynamic teacher I knew and loved—have sold out so easily? (Don't worry, Bill—I came around.)

Sitting in his classroom, I saw the same Bill I had taught alongside. He had dynamic instruction, enjoyed a strong rapport with his students, and had created an engaging learning environment. After I observed him teaching, I asked him what he thought about the textbook and the approach the school was taking to curriculum. Confidently, he said he absolutely loved it. He shared that it allowed him to allocate his time in other ways, letting him focus on things he found even more powerful than curating and creating everything he used in his class.

Here was an educator I deeply respected, using canned content in an effective way that worked for him. My takeaway was that canned curriculum can be used in a successful way; it depends on your instructional approach. If a canned curriculum is used solely as a script, you are forgetting the human quality of education—what likely drew you to it in the first place. Watching Bill made me realize that the tool or resource is not inherently bad; however, the implementation of the resource could be hindering some powerful learning and teaching. You must be careful about how you implement these prepacked, canned resources.

Administrators need to invest in finding ways to help teachers grow together rather than forcing them to be the same. A curriculum mapping process should guide teachers to be thoughtful about what resources they are using to help students master skills; it should not be a list of items to be used without question. The teacher's role is to decide how to use these tools. A high-quality resource that is effective for one teacher and his or her classroom might not necessarily fit into the learning environment or style of another. Efforts should be made to help teachers sharpen their individual craft. This honors all of them as creators and professionals. When teachers feel supported and that they have been given the space to grow, resources themselves won't seem like enemies.

I often hear the idea of "complete teacher creativity" met with this argument: students should get a similar educational experience within a district or school regardless of who their instructors are. For example, if one student has math with Mrs. S and another student has math with Mr. B, both students should be exposed to the same experiences. Of course students should be supported in their learning, and parents should have high expectations for the learning process regardless of the teacher, but parents can't expect all instructors to teach the same way. Instructors are not all the same! When teachers are asked to teach the same subject, in the same way, using the exact same resources, they are robbed of their ability to make the best decisions for the students in their classroom.

Here I must draw a line in the sand: teachers must be treated as professionals. When I left the classroom to become a technology coach, friends and family members frequently asked me two questions:

- Are you essentially working yourself out of a job?
- Do you think eventually computers will replace teachers?

The short answer to both of those questions is No! First, I can't work myself out of a constantly evolving job. As a technology coach, I wouldn't be doing a good job if my job didn't change. If I never moved beyond training on technology tools to talking about blended learning, I would be ineffective. Every year my job is radically different. This is how it should be. Second, teachers can't be replaced by computers—ever.

If our communities believe teachers have to be the same to support their students with equally high-quality education, they are buying into the idea that teaching isn't human. If people want all students learning the exact same way, they are asking teachers to be less than human. Educators teaching from entirely different curricula is a problem, but I don't think this is what educators are asking for. They are asking for the right to be who they are, use their personalities, and allow their students to know them as role models and as people.

When I was a college student, I worked in a school as a temporary secretary and had the opportunity to fill in for the high school secretary, who had to take a leave of absence. One day as a visitor waited to meet with the assistant principal (AP), we made small talk and realized we had a mutual friend. Later in the day, the AP asked me not to make small talk with the visitors waiting in the office. I instinctively replied that it was my personality to speak with someone when left alone with them, instead of sitting in awkward silence. I was advised to "use less of my personality." (Of course, it wasn't until years later that I thought of the perfect response to this.) I thought I had been doing a decent job, and I've never forgotten my strange interaction with the AP. Why was the office expected to be a cold place of business, without interaction with visitors?

WHEN TEACHERS FEEL SUPPORTED AND THAT THEY HAVE BEEN GIVEN THE SPACE TO GROW, RESOURCES THEMSELVES WON'T SEEM LIKE ENEMIES.

. . . .

Relating to others as part of your profession should be considered a positive. I'm not suggesting that you forget boundaries and be a completely "open book" for your students. Any past student of mine will tell you I believe in professional relationship. In fact, I use the word inappropriate quite often. It is one of my favorite words, and I probably use it to the point of annoyance. My students knew this about me—and teased me about it. For a few years, I was an assistant throwing coach for our high school girls track team. One year the team "decorated" my yard at night, covering the grass with donuts (my husband is a cop) and stringing toilet paper from the trees. They even wrote, "Is this inappropriate?" in chalk on my driveway! They did this out of love, of course, and this is a fond memory. (The only point of sharing this story is to prove my overuse of the word inappropriate.) More to the actual point, however: What better way to infuse your strengths and personality "appropriately" into your profession than by creating your own materials based on your relationship with your students?

HOW CAN TEACHERS BE CREATIVE WHEN THEY'RE NOT SUPPORTED BY THEIR DISTRICTS?

Investing in one's classroom isn't a new concept. Teachers purchasing materials out of their own pockets is a well-known practice—to the point that they are able to claim a portion of these expenses on their taxes (albeit a small portion). Educators in any role follow this trend. I frequently purchase small items to gift to teachers to show my appreciation. Administrators regularly buy breakfast or lunch for their staff. Teachers purchase pens, art supplies, and bulletin board bobbles for their classrooms. One year, I had to purchase my own reams of paper because the school ran out for the semester. I think it's safe to say that most educators are eager to invest in their jobs in meaningful ways. Financial investment for extras isn't required, of course; it is a choice that teachers make as a way to invest in the success of their relationships with students and their class culture and environment. However, the primary role of classroom teachers is to instruct students, guiding them through the mastery of skills and coaching them through the practice of critical thinking. Who is responsible for ensuring that educators have what they need to execute these core functions?

The answer is simple: districts and schools should provide teachers with all they need to guide instruction. Why then do teachers feel forced to choose to invest personally in instructional materials specifically? Although school districts aren't requiring this or encouraging this (at least in my personal experience), it is a real issue.

When you look at how often teachers feel they need to purchase materials for their courses to be creative, save time, or fill gaps in the resources they have, it becomes clear that districts are missing something. I have to wonder what is broken in our educational system. Districts go through curriculum processes, unwrap standards, and design pacing guides. They evaluate and adopt textbooks, digital curriculum, and supplemental materials. Yet teachers in our country still feel they aren't being properly supported.

Teachers' responsibilities have changed dramatically, but district and school structures, in many cases, have not. The resources they give teachers haven't changed much either, beyond expanding to digital spaces.

Some schools do pay teachers stipends to write curriculum, but often they're only given a short time period to do this, possibly working for two weeks over the summer to write a course. While this is a giant step toward reinvesting in teachers and treating them as instructional designers, it still does not send the message that curriculum is fluid and living. Without a thoughtful way to regularly revisit these materials, even this can easily become a "one and done" situation. If creating authentic and relevant instructional materials is a priority for schools, they have to regularly embed this as part of what teachers do every day.

IF CREATING AUTHENTIC AND RELEVANT INSTRUCTIONAL MATERIALS IS A PRIORITY FOR SCHOOLS, THEY HAVE TO REGULARLY EMBED THIS AS PART OF WHAT TEACHERS DO EVERY DAY.

• • • • • • • • • • •

How can districts and schools support teachers as designers? I believe it starts with how they view time. Never having enough time is a completely real challenge to overcome in schools; however, it also can be an easy excuse to fall back on. Schools must change how they use time. They cannot simply accept that there is never enough time—never enough time to grade, offer professional development, and collaborate with colleagues.

When I was doing my undergraduate work, a friend of mine asked what I was currently reading. At the time, I wasn't reading anything for pleasure (totally abnormal for me), so I responded that I had been busy with school and hadn't found the time to read. I've never forgotten his reply: "There is always time to read." This has become a personal mantra. People make time for what is important to them. It should be a priority for schools to invest in their teachers in such a way as to allow them to explore, remix, and create incredible learning experiences for students. This is a call to action: if schools truly view teacher creation as a priority, they have to be willing to make it one.

What if teachers had time to design built into their schedule every day? What if design days were woven into their teacher contracts? Imagine that you come to school one day simply to create for your class. The day might start with a quick five-minute thought prompt—something to keep in mind as you design. For example, your school might encourage you to focus on teacher interaction. But five minutes is all—no additional professional development on this day. You spend the rest of the day creating, perhaps with some built-in structures to encourage you to work across the curriculum or with another teacher in your content area.

Districts and schools must view teachers as instructional designers. Beyond supporting them to create the best materials for their classrooms, as schools expand into digital spaces, teachers also need to know how to design materials so they can truly vet online resources. Recently a high school principal and I talked about where his teachers were going to find content online. He asked my opinion about a certain platform, and I shared that teachers must evaluate online items in the same way we ask students to evaluate sources as they research. Of course, teachers do this naturally, but I'm not sure they are always asking themselves the full scope of questions as they quickly evaluate. Can I use this resource? Can I modify this resource? Is this resource accessible? Should I use this resource?

My point is that teachers can't fully evaluate content if they aren't supported in evaluating their own design skills. Conversely, if they become pros at evaluating content, they can naturally transition into designing it. From my perspective, teachers aren't empowered to see themselves as instructional designers. However, they fall into this role and are left to tackle it largely on their own. None of the schools I've worked in have supported me through time or resources to help me understand what open educational resources are, where to find them, how to use them, or how to apply best practices for designing digital content.

Teachers are doing the absolute best they can every day. This is not a criticism of them. This is a call to action for districts and schools to better support their teachers. If they see that teachers are struggling under pressure to create—regardless of the factors putting them in this situation—districts and schools must ask themselves why, and seek ways to provide the needed support.

HOW CAN TEACHERS CREATE WHEN THEY FEAR FAILURE?

If I am being honest, failure isn't something I handle well. I am not immune to its effects. Risk-taking and learning from failure did not come easily—which is still something I have to stay aware of.

When I was eighteen, my parents threw me an awesome party to celebrate my high school graduation. My mom ordered beautiful invitations with my school colors, and we picked out matching thank you cards. After the party, I set to work writing the thank you notes, and I wanted them to be perfect. I wanted the words I chose to truly capture how I was feeling. I deeply appreciated my family and friends celebrating with me and sending me off to college with such warm wishes. But I was also sad because this was my first milestone not shared with my grandfather. He and I were incredibly close, and his passing still felt fresh. These two things created a strange pressure I placed on myself. I wanted the cards to be personalized so each person would understand how much they meant to me. I started writing the notes one by one. Gradually, I picked away at the stack, working on a few each day. When I felt one wasn't good enough, I ripped it up and started over. As time went on, I convinced myself none of them were good enough. Ultimately, I never sent them—any of them. My parents were so upset with me. A family member asked me about it months later, and I was embarrassed. Even after all of this time, I still feel terribly guilty about it.

What I couldn't verbalize as an eighteen-year-old makes complete sense to me now. I had placed so much pressure on myself to create perfect mementos of thanks, I essentially paralyzed myself. Now I recognize this as fear of failure. Instead of just writing the notes—imperfect though they might have been—I never completed them at all.

This fear of failure—this paralysis of perfection—is a constant struggle for me. I imagine, as creators, you have these moments as well. How often do you transfer these fears into your work? How can you design when you fear failing?

I would suggest that you can't. To break the rules of education through creativity and design, teachers must give up any aspirations of perfection. Even if you don't have all of the kinks worked out in a newly created lesson, give it a go. Upload your first instructional video to YouTube, even if you aren't yet an editing pro. In fact, don't edit that video at all: just be the you that your students know and love.

Waiting for the perfect concept or discarding anything less than ideal only impedes creativity. Only when teachers aren't afraid of failing can they fully embrace designing. (Oh, and if you attended my high school graduation party in the summer of 2003—thank you!)

THE PAYOFF

At this point, you may be wrestling with conflicting emotions. You may be excited about the relationship you have with your students and about designing materials based on their specific interests and needs. But you also may be asking yourself whether you're willing to embark on a potentially more difficult path than the one you've taken previously. Designing—from scratch, a template, or using other resources—is harder than working with a script or canned curriculum. If it is harder, why would you take this path? Because the payoff for all of your efforts is tremendous.

Recently I was criticized for a blended learning initiative I was working on with a team. Someone asked me, "Why are you encouraging us to do it in this way when this way seems so much harder than what other schools might be doing?" In the moment, I gave a long-winded response, but it didn't get to the heart of the answer. Why do people do something the hard way when it could be easier? Honestly, they do it because they want to do the right thing and, as the age-old truth states, doing the right thing is usually harder. In this example, the team was trying something new together, and more often than not, new things feel hard at first. For an online lesson, it might be easier to post a digital worksheet and be done with it, but that isn't the right thing to do for students.

Furthermore, considering copyright when designing and remixing might feel to some like just another thing to worry about, thus making our jobs harder. Creating instructional materials through a lens of copyright both encourages responsible creation AND is the right thing to do. Not only is doing the right thing never wrong, but when designing instructional materials, considering copyright can be leverage for student benefit. Frankly, considering and trying something new—if it is reflective and focuses on improving student learning—isn't an argument educators should be having. Although we might have strong opinions on which strategies work best, we should all agree that constant reflection and improvement is part of embodying lifelong learning.

CREATING INSTRUCTIONAL MATERIALS THROUGH A LENS OF COPYRIGHT BOTH ENCOURAGES RESPONSIBLE CREATION AND IS THE RIGHT THING TO DO.

Designing courses and digital resources can improve your face-to-face teaching every day. And if you look at the coursework required for preservice educators, odds are you won't find instructional design as a prerequisite for student teaching. The typical PD schedule doesn't always allow for much time. Designing, curating, and remixing content can help you grow as an instructor, and districts must be willing to put in the time and resources necessary for this to become a reality.

Educators are asked to do so much more than the general public even knows. They do it all, and they do it well because they believe in the work they do. But they can't run on fumes, and they can't continue to pull magic out of empty hats. Teachers are magical, but their power only goes so far, and they have to conserve some of that power to use outside of their classrooms, too. Those in leadership roles must take a hard look at the process for building a pool of resources—whatever those resources might be—in a way to support teachers, give them time to figure things out, and build their capacity to become designers of high-quality content.

If educators are expecting students to create and produce to show learning, educators must be willing to do the same. Most classroom teachers recognize that teaching has shifted so that the role of the teacher has changed. Active learning encourages teachers to take the role of lead learner, helping their students navigate and explore. But teachers also must be willing to continue to learn, be inspired, and create right along with their students. Building their own content and instructional materials is the perfect approach to this end. In this scenario, teachers are learning, creating, considering intellectual property, contributing to the pool of resources, and helping other educators in the crazy, rough sea of education. They are learning about good design and sharpening their pedagogical skills. They are collaborating, getting real feedback, and considering their learners.

DECISIONS GUIDED BY DATA—THE STEADY BASS LINE

When you have control over what you use in your classroom, you can tailor it to your students and to yourself. You can consider student interests, relevant topics, your personality, stories from life, challenges in your community, etc. Regardless of whether you are intentional about it, you are constantly collecting all types of data from your students. In turn, you can use this information to thoughtfully leverage the materials you select, the materials you create, and the overall learning environment you create.

You also can use hard data to inform the design of your lessons. If a gap exists in the resources you have and a skill you need to address for your students, you can confidently fill the gap with high-quality materials. Additionally, blended learning is most powerful when you use student data to inform your decisions about materials, groupings, and pathways. You can also allow your students to analyze their own data to make decisions about their learning.

Designing content helps you become a better instructor because you have been part of the process from beginning to end. You can craft, recraft, reflect, and revisit. In this way, you not only explore the map, you also create it. Because of this, you know where the tricky roads are, the detours you might have to make, and the attractions worth stopping for.

FLEXIBILITY

When you create something from scratch or use materials you have permission to modify, you have the flexibility to continually revise and update the content. When Kanye West pulled his stunt on Taylor Swift, interrupting her as she received her 2009 MTV Video Music Award, you'd better believe I used the reference in my materials. But after a while the reference got stale, so I replaced it with something more immediately relevant. When you control what your materials look like, they can be growing, living, and breathing resources instead of being chiseled into stone and marked with an expiration date.

Every year you learn more about your craft. You've heard about teachers with thirty years of experience who have done the same lessons every year for the last thirty years, changing nothing about the resources, teaching practices, or learning environment. Some make the argument that these teachers actually have only one year of experience because they did not embrace a growth mindset and were not intentionally flexible. Most educators do not have a fixed mindset, but they have to choose learning and flexibility every day. You got into this profession because you love learning, and you continue to see yourself as a student of your profession. You see each unit, day, semester, quarter, and year as a new start—a chunk of time you can reflect on, learn from, and use to improve. Most educators I have learned from are serious and active participants in their own constant personal growth, barely finishing an activity before launching into how they might improve it the next time. While living in a constantly revolving space may seem tiring, it's the only way you can continually grow.

WHEN YOU CONTROL WHAT YOUR MATERIALS LOOK LIKE, THEY CAN BE GROWING, LIVING, AND BREATHING RESOURCES INSTEAD OF BEING CHISELED INTO STONE AND MARKED WITH AN EXPIRATION DATE.

. . . .

DEVELOPMENT OF PERSONAL SKILLS

As I was working with a group of teachers and their curriculum director in 2018, the group found some significant gaps in how one of their recently adopted curricular programs covered skills and standards. After they worked to identify the gaps, they were going to collaborate to create units to support students as they learned and mastered those specific skills. Their plan was to collaboratively build hyperdocs and use these as units and activities to be woven into the current adopted resources. My role was to facilitate a PD session to introduce what hyperdocs are and talk about how we would use this process to build openly licensed, thoughtful digital materials, through the process of creating hyperdocs. The goal was to support teachers as they created a digital instructional design plan and executed it so it became a package for student learning.

During our training session, one teacher asked, "If I can find something already done online, can't I just use that?" Good question. Why reinvent something existing already, especially if you are strapped for time or someone has already done it better than you think you can? But the goal of this particular initiative wasn't for the teachers simply to use hyperdocs with their students. The goal was to help them become content curators and creators, and to empower them to see themselves as such. The long-term goal was for teachers to explore how to vet high-quality resources they find online, leverage those resources to design incredible learning experiences for students, create interactive digital learning, and ultimately design blended and technology-enhanced content.

The long-term goals were certainly worthy of the effort; however, without fully understanding these goals, some quickly translated the hyperdoc plan into "Let's do more work!" In reality, if we work to improve our skills related to searching for, vetting, remixing, and creating content, those skills ultimately will allow us to work smarter—not harder.

CHAPTER 4

Educators as Designers

LAY DOWN SOME TRACKS

What does it mean to be a teacher today? Depending on who answers this question, the definitions will vary. Non-educators seem to have strong opinions about what educators do, what they think educators should do better, and what they think educators should do more or less of. But how do *educators* define teaching? Their definition is what matters; they are the ones who have lived it. The role of an educator is dynamic and complicated. Over time, the title of "teacher" has shifted to "facilitator," and educators have heard the cry to change their practice from one of "sage on the stage" to that of "guide on the side."

I like to think of educators as creators and designers of learning experiences. This is the craft they continue to sharpen year after year, and during the experience, educators are involved in all aspects of the design. They choose, modify, and create resources. They build in procedures, support students in their role as learners, and help students advocate for their own learning. Being a creator and designer doesn't mean you have to bust out the macaroni noodles and "craft" your students to death (although I was totally called out by students for this during my student teaching!). You can be creative in a lot of ways, and you can choose your approach to make it truly your own.

Some definitely don't believe educators are properly trained to be instructional designers. Those critics might say teachers do not have the knowledge base or time to both design and deliver instructional content.

They might say it is unrealistic to think these educators should be asked to design content. Perhaps some of this is true. I'd imagine that most educators would agree they don't have enough time to design everything they use in class from scratch; however, the truth is that educators are often designing content. They are curating, remixing, and designing content and learning experiences. They search the best sites they know of to find items to make it easier to build this content. They don't really have a choice. In fact, those who say teachers aren't creating content haven't been in classrooms recently, or they would know this is what teachers do today.

Regardless of whether educators call themselves "instructional designers," their jobs require them to design. In my undergraduate experience, which I started over fifteen years ago, preservice educators were asked to design. We designed lesson plans, student projects, and activities for students to interact with. However, none of the guidance I was given during that time made me feel qualified to consider myself an instructional designer. Your own preparation to be a teacher may not have "trained" you to think like an instructional designer, but you probably find yourself learning on the job. And some have more on-the-job training than others.

NO MATTER THEIR ROLE, EDUCATORS DESIGN CONTENT AND EXPERIENCES CONSTANTLY.

The role of the designer isn't limited to those in the classroom working directly with students. No matter their role, educators design content and experiences constantly. Administrators work with teams to design and deliver professional development. Superintendents work with teams to design school visions and goals. Educators create strategic plans. They revise and revisit. They create evaluation tools. They design master schedules. Literally, everything they do is a creation—whether they are creating items from scratch or not. How often have you discovered something in your district created from scratch? How often have you found a modification of something another school uses or a combination of several resources put together in a way relevant to your school or district? We borrow language and ideas from other school districts. We see the power in being able to modify these resources so they make the most sense in our situations and with our communities. We see the value in adding autonomy and personality. We brand these items as our own. From superintendent to student population, everyone in education is a designer and must consider what message is sent when creative powers are not applied appropriately.

"Achieve" with an Authentic Curriculum
-MICHELE EATON-

When you design, remix, or rework instructional content, you deliver it better because you believe in it, understand it, and know it from creation to implementation. Michele Eaton is the director of virtual and blended learning for the Municipal School District (M.S.D.) of Wayne Township in Indianapolis, Indiana. Michele speaks to the power of teachers as instructional designers and how this approach has impacted classrooms in her schools.

Much of the work she does guides teachers through the process of designing courses for Achieve Virtual Education Academy, a public high school serving students entirely virtually. When Achieve Virtual was born, they made the decision to provide unique, local, and authentic courses designed by Indiana educators rather than to purchase canned courses. This model has been wildly successful for them.

Michele explains: "What makes us unique in the state is our teachers write all of our courses. We believe our teachers should have ownership of the content they are teaching, and one of the best ways to do this is to have them design it."

Teachers at Achieve Virtual design courses almost completely by using Open Educational Resources and do not adopt any traditional textbooks unless they are legally required for the course. Michele is charged with supporting teachers through this process and provides personalized professional learning around digital content curation and instructional design. Michele speaks to how this model builds a skillset for teachers while providing authentic learning experiences for students:

"We have the ability to not be so rigid in how we teach. We can offer individualized and personalized content. Often, you don't have that flexibility with a canned curriculum. A lot of products say that you can have flexibility, and what that usually means is that you can take things out, not necessarily remix or add in your own content."

The model Achieve Virtual uses is a model that traditional schools can learn from, too. Technology-enhanced classrooms and blended classrooms must consider high-quality design of digital content. Achieve Virtual has become a catalyst for this positive change in the traditional classrooms of Wayne Township as well.

"The benefit of this we didn't necessarily plan on is that when you have been doing online and blended learning for several years, you have teachers who are trained in instructional design and Open Educational Resources [OER] working alongside teachers in traditional classrooms. We have seen what our blended and virtual teachers are learning [OER and digital design] transfer to traditional classrooms as well. It has been cool to see digital content being curated and designed in high-quality, meaningful ways."

Achieve Virtual pays their teachers to write and teach courses, demonstrating the importance of investing in this process. Michele acknowledges that designing high-quality content is time-consuming and tough. This is why she is so passionate about supporting adult learning surrounding this topic.

"We need to admit that instructional design is a new teacher skillset. Every teacher needs to have this skill. We work to give students access to devices, and we encourage the creation of digital content. We deliver this content to students through learning management systems. We need to be more intentional about helping educators grow as instructional designers and having conversations about how we learn differently online."

CHAPTER 5
Using Edtech in Design

To design digital content, you don't have to be a "techie teacher." In fact, the techie teacher myth is one you should put to rest. "Techie teachers" don't exist; some teachers are simply okay with trying new things and potentially stumbling and searching a bit until they figure it out. I am not discounting that technology comes more easily to some than to others, but being a strong instructor has little to do with how easily technology comes to you.

Think of exploring technology tools as a way to be creative in your instructional design. The more you try new tools and strategies, the more likely you are to design authentic and interactive digital content.

Skills inspire ideas. Isn't this what we are hoping to do for our students—give them the skills they need to create new products and solutions to problems? Regardless of how you work toward becoming proficient in the use of technology, no one can tell you how to implement these tools in your classroom. Instead, PD should empower you to make those decisions yourself, because you have the knowledge base and resources to draw from.

LEARNING NEW INSTRUMENTS

Many paths and resources are available to boost your confidence in the use of technology tools and to support you in creating and curating resources. The Google Level One certification is a great place to start. Although it won't necessarily train you to become an instructional designer, it will give you the tools to start exploring. Through exploring the tools, you apply the skills and attempt things you may not have tried before. The process of becoming Google Level One Certified won't spark your creative motivation unless you choose to do something with it and let the process inspire you.

As a tech coach, I was constantly reminded of the huge line between focusing on technology and focusing on learning. At first glance, when prepping to take the Google Level 1 or Level 2 Educator Exam, it might seem to be simply focused on how to use the tools; however, it is much more dynamic. The process can inspire you to find both practical and innovative solutions for creation and collaboration as you become proficient in using each GSuite tool. If your students use GSuite as their creative suite of tools, I highly encourage you to become a certified educator. As you learn the features of the tools, you will be inspired to create. Educators naturally acquire ideas for the classroom just moving through life. You might see a movie clip and know the perfect place to use it. You might read an article in the paper and immediately a related lesson comes to mind. Going through the Google Level 1 or Level 2 Educator Exam prep process is very much the same. Knowing the features of Google Forms might inspire you to create a Choose Your Own Adventure experience for your students to use in a blended learning environment. Knowing your way around Google Slides might encourage you to show students how to design social media posts for a storytelling exercise. The point of the process isn't to shine a light on the tools; it shines a light on what the tools can do and how you can leverage them in your classroom for learning—specifically, how they can help you design learning experiences for your students.

THINK OF EXPLORING TECHNOLOGY TOOLS AS A WAY TO BE CREATIVE IN YOUR INSTRUCTIONAL DESIGN.

You will never be able to keep up with every new technology tool created, so try what works for you. When you explore the tools available to support you in creating, delivering, and designing content for your students, you will immediately discover a potentially crowded and chaotic world. So many tools are available! How do you make the right choice? If you are flexible and allow your learning objectives to drive what you are doing in your class, you will most likely discover a tool to support your goals. If you are open to taking a risk and willing to try something new without fear of failure, your skillset as a designer of learning experiences will grow. Educators talk often of technology being "another tool in your toolbox," but they need to remember the toolbox should also include design and curation tools. A "technology toolbox" is more than simply the nuts and bolts to put learning into motion. Inside a fully stocked teacher toolbox, you will find paint, paintbrushes, blank canvases, and maybe even some glitter!

Don't let the tools dictate what you do. You can get creative within any system in which you are asked to work. Whatever learning management system (LMS) your district uses, make it work for you. If yours is not a GSuite school, chances are, you good that youchances are, you can use different tools to accomplish the same strategies and ideas. Apple? Google? Microsoft? It really doesn't matter (though I'm a Google girl myself!). Focus on strategies for learning and high-quality learning experiences. Be inventive about how technology tools can support your design!

INFORMATION LITERACY AND DIGITAL CITIZENSHIP—THE RELIABLE RHYTHM

You are out to dinner with friends, and a question comes up that sparks a healthy debate. Bam! You pull out your cell phone and settle it with some quick—what I like to call "casual"—research. You find the first source supporting your viewpoint, and poof! Debate won! This is how casual research is done! The first road trip I took with my husband was before we had smartphones. A lengthy car ride lended itself to long conversations and debates. I remember one of us saying we needed to be able to bring a computer with us to solve our "debates." Today people have access to information whenever they want it and for any purpose. (And just for the record, I was always "right" in our debates. Now I can just prove it faster! And poor, abused Google! If you haven't watched the CollegeHumor YouTube series of videos titled "If Google Was a Guy," take a moment to see what I mean. But fair warning, the videos are not school appropriate.)

"Casual research" has its place. If I have part of a song in my head but I can't quite figure out what it is, I can use Google to solve the mystery with the smallest fraction of a lyric. Quite frankly, this enriches my life. Likely most people can think of a specific instance when Google saved them long hours of frustration from trying to force their brain to recall something they just had to know "right now." Again, casual research has its place—but it's not in all classroom scenarios.

Academic research requires more concrete skills, whether they are being used to write a formal paper or as part of a less traditional assignment.

Mastering and applying informational literacy skills within their learning and creation is critical for students. Informational literacy includes all of the skills necessary to locate, evaluate, and effectively use material. All educators, regardless of their content area, are responsible for integrating these skills into learning.

In a technology-rich learning environment, students are required to build literacy skills of several types. From digital literacy to media literacy, information literacy ties together much of what students do online. Information literacy also can be applied in building teachers as creators. It asks the same questions of teachers they would ask of their students in applying these skills, falling under the same umbrella of copyright, digital citizenship, etc.

Building a digital curriculum supports informational literacy skills for teachers in three specific ways:

Locating sources (research) is the first piece of information literacy. Teachers have been trained in the art of beg, borrow, and steal. Teachers truly cannot create literally every single item from scratch, so the first step is to "locate" or research. Where do teachers go to quickly and efficiently search for instructional materials? Pinterest? A quick Google search? Or are better ways to locate class resources available?

The second piece of information literacy is **evaluating sources and information**. Part of this is achieved when you become skilled in locating sources and information. But how do you build the skills needed to evaluate resources to determine whether you should be using them or not? Source evaluation includes looking for bias, relevancy, date of publication, etc.

Effectively using the information is the third piece of information literacy. As teachers locate resources, evaluate them for quality, and find a meaningful way to use them—while protecting intellectual property—we see new products being created. Ultimately, teachers want their students to have the same skills: the ability to think critically about what they explore and to build new and exciting ideas prompted by it. Using the information correctly also includes applying citations and, when applicable, knowledge of copyright.

Naturally embedding information literacy into what you do every day as an educator gives you a meaningful, just-in-time approach to tackling and mastering an essential skill you are called to pass on to your students. Information literacy, digital citizenship, and copyright are under the same umbrella for building students who know how to live, create, and interact in online spaces.

ULTIMATELY, TEACHERS WANT THEIR STUDENTS TO HAVE THE SAME SKILLS: THE ABILITY TO THINK CRITICALLY ABOUT WHAT THEY EXPLORE AND TO BUILD NEW AND EXCITING IDEAS PROMPTED BY IT.

• • • • • • • • • • •

Copyright overlaps with themes you should be teaching within digital citizenship as well. Respecting intellectual and creative property and doing the right thing when we are monitoring ourselves is core to digital citizenship. Schools have a tendency to oversimplify digital citizenship, but it is a complex and dynamic subject. It makes sense to focus on cyberbullying as a priority within digital citizenship, but this is only one element of it. I've also heard some educators claim that digital citizenship is simply an extension of citizenship in general. Although this might be true in some respects, adding a new landscape of an online space does present unique challenges and opportunities that educators must address directly and not dismiss. Digital citizenship and a thoughtful approach to copyright in the classroom both ask educators to follow the law—being responsible in their use of content, being respectful in their interactions with others, communicating effectively, and following etiquette. Ignoring copyright in your classroom while trying to encourage students to be good digital citizens doesn't send a clear message to your students. Rather, it communicates that students can choose when to consider these things and when to ignore them. Honoring copyright is not something you can choose; it must always be important, not just when you decide to acknowledge it.

CIPA AND COPPA

In the first year that my current district was a 1:1 district, starting with grades nine through twelve, the most immediate feedback we heard from teachers was that they thought the devices were no more than expensive pencils (not a new analogy to us in edtech) because they felt, at every turn, something they wanted students to have access to was blocked by the filters put in place by the school. At the start of our second year, we believed it was important to have a direct conversation about why the practice of Internet filtering was done and to open a dialogue about how to best serve the instructional needs of our staff to support the best possible learning environment for our students. The result was one of my very favorite PD sessions I delivered in partnership with Chris Bowers, technology director at the district during that time. In our conversation, we started by addressing the topic of the Children's Internet Protection Act (CIPA), the Children's Online Privacy Protection Act (COPPA), and Terms of Service.

According to the Federal Communications Commission (FCC), CIPA "was enacted by Congress in 2000 to address concerns about children's access to obscene or harmful content over the Internet."[1] Essentially, the act requires all schools receiving E-Rate funding to create and implement an Internet safety policy addressing the following, paraphrased from the FCC:

- Access to inappropriate online content
- Student safety when using forms of digital communication
- Hacking and other illegal online behaviors
- Protection of minors' personal information
- Restricted access to harmful content[2]

The E-Rate funding program is central to schools being able to provide access to students. The Universal Service Administrative Company (USAC) is a nonprofit organization that was created in 1997 with a goal of making Internet services more affordable to schools and libraries.[3] This program can offer up to a ninety percent discount for telecommunications and Internet access. Chances are, your school is eligible for and applies for E-Rate support, and it has to agree to the stipulations outlined in CIPA to maintain E-Rate status. Although this might seem like you are simply ticking the boxes to keep your discount, the reality is that schools should be offering this support simply because it is the right thing to do.

Teachers responded very positively to our PD presentation, because we were opening up the conversation and focusing on why decisions had been made to filter the Internet in the way we were operating. It is nearly impossible for technology leaders to filter in a way to make every person happy. Everyone seems to have strong opinions about how filtering should be done in educational spaces.

When we first went 1:1 with Chromebooks in my current district, Kahoot! was an incredibly popular tool to use with students. In fact, it is such a great tool, I suspect students across the country were "Kahoot!ed" to death for awhile. (No judgment here. If I find a new tool I love, I use it like crazy. If I hear a new song I love, I listen to it on repeat for weeks.) As I walked through the halls, I heard the Kahoot! song playing like a medley of slot machines in a Vegas casino. One day well into the year, Kahoot! was accidentally recategorized by our web filter, and students no longer had access to it. Although fixing this was easy, watching how it unfolded was interesting. Teachers were eager to come to Kahoot!'s defense and explain the value of the tool. They were ready to fight for access to it, not realizing the change was made by a bot, and no one had manually taken access away.

Working with a director who made these topics a priority and weighed them in every decision made for the corporation was incredibly influential to developing the Copyrighteous mentality. We create responsibly with student learning in mind, and we responsibly provide resources to students so they can create.

TERMS OF SERVICE AND A DIGITAL COMING OF AGE

In educational technology, the age of thirteen is a big deal. This is the magical age opening the door to a plethora of technology tools previously unavailable to the preteen. Quite literally, turning thirteen is a digital coming of age.

In reality, we know students have access to and are using apps on a daily basis that they are technically too young for. I'm not suggesting that age is the best factor for deciding when an individual is ready to be exposed to something. However, educators have a legal and ethical responsibility to model digital citizenship and honor the system in place to protect their students. Digital citizenship is not simply making items off limits for students based on age, the possibility of distraction, or exposure to content. Instead, it is supporting students in the building of skills so when they are faced with a decision of what to access, they can navigate the choice guided by self-regulation.

QUITE LITERALLY, TURNING THIRTEEN IS A DIGITAL COMING OF AGE.

• • • • • • • • • • •

The phrases "can do" and "should do" are two very different things. Can you log in to your home HBO account to show your students a movie? Yes, you can do this—but should you? On the first day of school one year, I decided to ask my students to write down one band or song representing their musical taste. I collected all the submissions and used them to create a classroom Pandora station. Whenever we needed to listen to music in the classroom, I played the custom Pandora station—the strange, eclectic mix of each class. I thought it was a great idea! Sometimes, we tried to guess which band or song must have influenced the soundtrack in a particular direction. It served a purpose in the classroom, allowing us to connect and share our personal interests.

Fast forward a few years to the moment I sat in front of the interview panel for my first official job in edtech. I don't remember the question prompting me to share this classroom experience, but as I told them about our classroom custom Pandora stations, I saw the technology director and the curriculum director share a knowing smile. Months later, as this same technology director mentored me by helping me build my understanding of topics such as Terms of Service, I had an epiphany. I had essentially confessed my Terms of Service "sins" in front of an entire interview panel of educators! Pandora's Terms of Service—like many other streaming services—do not allow us to use personal Pandora accounts the way I had.

Critics will say, "Go on with your bad self! You listen to those Pandora stations!" Or fill in the blank with whatever technology tool you want to use but were told you "can't." This likely isn't the right approach. By contrast, if educators aren't careful, they could take this far too seriously and end up living in a sterile world where they are afraid to get dirty. This approach probably isn't best either. Striking the right balance between breaking the rules and following them is the perfect place to be mindful about copyright, digital citizenship, and terms of use. Let your learning experiences for your students break the rules of education while responsibly choosing the tools they are utilizing.

My hope is you have support in your building and district so you don't have to allocate a ton of time to reading the Terms of Service for every technology tool you use. However, if your "support" comes in the form of merely blocking access to tools with no conversation as to why, this is an opportunity to ask questions, learn, and potentially adjust. If you happen to be in a position to make filtering decisions, I encourage you to connect with classroom teachers to share your work—an open line of communication makes a big difference. And my final bone to pick: if you regularly present on edtech topics, please take the time to understand the Terms of Service for the tools you are promoting so that your sharing is responsible.

OTHER EDTECH CONSIDERATIONS

Focus on the objective instead of the tool. When you design learning experiences based on a new technology tool you hear about, you run the risk of placing an inauthentic product at the heart of your goal instead of being focused on student learning. This is sort of a chicken-before-the-egg scenario. As an edtech professional, the right thing is to always focus on the learning goal first and then find a tool to make it happen. I completely stand by this advice, but there is a little bit of power in letting a tool guide you to the space where those sound pedagogical ideas happen, too.

Think about it this way: you hear about the best new tool for collaboration for students, allowing them to use video to share their ideas and reflections. This tool is incredibly popular, and while it might be trendy and some might even call it a passing trend, it is allowing students to share and create in a way both manageable for teachers and approachable for all. Your first reaction to hearing about this tool might be, "Oh cool! My students can make a video!" But then you naturally start to ask the right questions:

- Why?
- How might I use this tool to help my students share their ideas?
- What ideas will they share?
- On what will I ask them to reflect?

Once your internal dialogue starts (and hopefully becomes a conversation among educators, making the idea even better!), it might even lead you to select an entirely different tool. When you focus on the learning objectives and choose the tool at the end of the process, you stay true to your why of student learning. When this is your process, the tool doesn't matter at all. You can be flexible about what tools you put into place to support your students in learning and creation.

But what if the new tool is only for those older than age thirteen? Does this mean you completely ditch the idea? Not at all! If you can get creative, you can find a way to make it happen. Luckily, the companies creating tools with students as the intended user are thinking about all of this, too. Look for tools with the Student Privacy Pledge or iKeepSafe partners to easily locate products making student privacy and safety a priority.

Find a way to make a different tool function in the same way. Do you want to give your students a writing opportunity that a blog would be perfect for? Does your favorite blogging platform state it is only for students above the age of thirteen? If you are staying true to this belief, that the tool itself shouldn't drive student learning, then shifting to a new tool because of safety and privacy should be easy to do. Turn a Google Site or a Google Slides presentation into a blog environment for students. Your students are still able to blog, student creation isn't prohibited because of the tool you chose, and you are considering the safest way for students to use tools.

Differing opinions exist about how schools can get parental permission. If you look at the Terms of Service of different sites disallowing use for anyone under the age of thirteen or even eighteen, you might see some language lending itself to permissible use if the parent or guardian gives permission. Although schools operate *in loco parentis*, some sites explicitly require parental permission. If students are not of age to enter into a legal contract (eighteen), then they must have parent permission.

What is the best solution to obtaining parent permission in these cases? Some schools send home a blanket permission slip, while others, based on legal guidance they are given, believe this isn't the best option. Some schools avoid this altogether by only using tools that make it easy for teachers to operate within the Terms of Service without getting any additional information. Some schools have permission slips to send home for each new tool introduced, which could become an organizational nightmare. If this isn't yet on your radar, who is the person you could reach out to who will support you through this process? Does your district or school have a policy for obtaining parental permission? If you are just getting started, you can take a step in the right direction by a quick CTRL + F search for age, 13, or 18 on any Terms of Service (or terms of use) page.

Provide this as a service to teachers. At its core, digital citizenship asks this question: Even if a tool is available to you, should you use it? Filtering the Internet is a polarizing conversation, to say the least. Some school districts choose to limit access to YouTube and social media platforms, whereas others prefer to offer support in the proper use of these sites. Wherever you fall on this spectrum, you must admit there is no perfect way to accomplish filtering student access in a way everyone agrees on. As an ever-changing and growing organism, the Internet cannot be contained. Even the most locked-down Internet filter may fail to prevent students from accessing tools and sites that are best to not have in their hands. Digital citizenship falls under the umbrella of responsibility of educators who live and learn in a digital space. Not only must you teach students how to use intellectual and creative property correctly, you should also support them to know what to access and what to avoid.

The way educators support students in all things digital citizenship (#digcit) varies from district to district, but integrating it into their learning cannot be overdone. All content areas and levels should be concerned with literacy, and the same applies to #digcit. It is the foundation for everything educators do online. Even if your school offers a #digcit course, digital citizenship skills can't be approached as a "one and done." Google's Be Internet Awesome curriculum, interactive Interland game, and Common Sense Education are my three favorite resources for integrating.

NOT ONLY MUST YOU TEACH STUDENTS HOW TO USE INTELLECTUAL AND CREATIVE PROPERTY CORRECTLY, YOU SHOULD ALSO SUPPORT THEM TO KNOW WHAT TO ACCESS AND WHAT TO AVOID.

· · · · · · · · · · ·

PART TWO: REPHRASE

Cover Songs

CHAPTER 6
Initiating the Remix

Maybe you already have materials you really love but wish you could make a couple of changes or make them more interactive. Understanding rules related to copyright, licensing, and fair use can help you determine whether you can make the changes you want to make. For example, how are the materials licensed? Have you considered the four factors of fair use? If you aren't sure how something is licensed, ask!

I recently worked with a high school teacher who wanted to deliver in a different format a resource she had purchased the rights to use. We weren't sure what the purchasing license allowed, so the teacher sent an email to the publisher. After a couple of email exchanges, the publisher granted her permission to remix and modify the resource as long as the only students using the materials were those currently in her class. If you aren't sure how you can use something you find—ask! One lesson I have learned in the copyright world is that no set of rules alone will ever provide the answer to every question.

Copyright, without a doubt, lives entirely in the gray space. I am not going to sugarcoat it. No infographic can comprehensively capture the rules of copyright to make them foolproof to follow. You have the road map, but you must be good at interpreting, readjusting, and making judgment calls; the rules just aren't that simple. I've seen the frustrated faces this provokes. When I first started focusing on copyright in the classroom, I created sessions to deliver at edtech conferences, usually designed with instructional coaches or other support personnel in mind. Teachers came to the sessions with very specific questions:

- Can I put this one thing I found online into my LMS?
- Can I download videos from this one digital resource?
- Can I scan this page and create a digital copy?

YOU HAVE THE ROAD MAP, BUT YOU MUST BE GOOD AT INTERPRETING, READJUSTING, AND MAKING JUDGMENT CALLS; THE RULES JUST AREN'T THAT SIMPLE.

• • • • • • • • • •

I could see they didn't leave with what they came to the session hoping to get. Unfortunately, I couldn't give concrete answers to those types of questions without more information or asking additional questions.

To navigate the gray space, I learned to ask myself additional questions to build the skills I needed to quickly run through this process on a case-by-case basis. You can also give yourself the tools to make the most informed decisions, but sometimes you have to ask for guidance. Again, if you aren't sure how a resource is licensed and you aren't sure what you can do with it, just ask.

DAVID WILEY'S 5 R'S FRAMEWORK

So, what is remixing? David Wiley introduced the 4R Framework[1] for the use of OER in 2007, and later added a fifth R in 2014. The heart of remixing reminds me of an old chant from dance camp: mix it, change it, rearrange it! Remixing celebrates the power of creating something new from the best resources you can find. Wiley coined the term "remixing" as part of this process and defined it as "the right to combine the original or revised content with other material to create something new (e.g., incorporate the content into a mashup)."

Although remixing is only part of breaking the rules of education and creating out-of-this-world experiences for your students, I'll argue it is the endgame. Remixing can be where transformative learning happens; it is the how and why combined. Remixing is part of the process of the OER movement. The entire scope of appropriate use and protection of intellectual and creative property for educators is outlined in the framework of the 5 R's.

1. *Retain*: the right to make, own, and control copies of the content (e.g., download, duplicate, store, and manage)
2. *Reuse*: the right to use the content in a wide range of ways (e.g., in a class, in a study group, on a website, in a video)
3. *Revise*: the right to adapt, adjust, modify, or alter the content itself (e.g., translate the content into another language)
4. *Remix*: the right to combine the original or revised content with other material to create something new (e.g., incorporate the content into a mashup)
5. *Redistribute*: the right to share copies of the original content, your revisions, or your remixes with others (e.g., give a copy of the content to a friend)

The goals of the framework are to:

- help educators understand how materials are licensed so they can properly attribute
- make it easier to find content labeled for reuse
- help educators be considerate and thoughtful in how they use the materials
- help educators apply licenses to their our own work so they can manage how their materials are used in the future
- promote sharing

Remixing is the art of creating new instructional resources specific to your teacher voice and the needs of your students. It's the new approach to the old "beg, borrow, and steal." Remixing is elevating our practice, shifting our process, and adding our personal touch. Remixing holds great power. It allows you to combine the best of both worlds: high-quality materials repackaged and delivered in your own voice.

This material is based on original writing by David Wiley, which was published freely under a Creative Commons Attribution 4.0 license at http://opencontent.org/definition.

REMIXING IS THE ART OF CREATING NEW INSTRUCTIONAL RESOURCES SPECIFIC TO YOUR TEACHER VOICE AND THE NEEDS OF YOUR STUDENTS.

• • • • • • • • • • •

The good news is that many educators are already doing this in their own way. Initially, this process involves finding materials and repackaging and remixing them so they work for your students and your classrooms. Teachers Google, Pinterest, and grab pieces of lessons they have done in the past. They might put these three items together in a digital activity for students within their LMS or repackage it into the form of a hyperdoc.

An improved way to remix is to shift where you find your resources and how you package them together. This improved process might take you to OER platforms to gather materials to remix in thoughtful ways. As you repackage your materials into something deliverable to students, you can then provide proper attributions for the resources you used. Finally, you can openly license your new resource when appropriate and share it out to be used and remixed by others.

As you learn where to go to find high-quality resources and take advantage of the #GoOpen movement, you become more efficient in the location of resources. When you become more proficient at locating resources, for example, you save time sifting through lower-quality resources or those less helpful in your classrooms. Learning how and where to find the best resources prevents you from becoming overwhelmed by too many unvetted resources and, instead, can direct you straight to the materials you can use and remix. When you combine your knowledge of copyright and fair use with the high-quality resources OER provides, your remixes can become viral hits—far better than an original ever could be.

This recipe includes knowing where to find openly licensed materials, how to apply fair use to the use of copyrighted materials, and how to repackage and remix these resources to create an engaging, interactive, and authentic experience for students.

Educators must understand copyright and appropriate use.

Educators must model appropriate use.

Educators must teach appropriate use.

START A BAND

Some teachers feel compelled to create their own materials. I fall into this camp for sure. However, teachers can't put themselves in a situation in which they are working alone in isolation. It isn't realistic for educators to expect themselves and others to make from scratch every single thing needed for students. But designing educational experiences doesn't require that everything be from scratch for it to be a unique experience, designed with you and your students in mind. If educators are honest, they must recognize that they each have strengths and weaknesses, and resources are available that they can use that exceed their content knowledge or design skills. They must let those high-quality materials and resources inform what they do. They then can leverage their personal learning networks (PLNs), their familiarity with OERs, and their critical eye to build high-quality experiences for their students. Although you have to become comfortable as a designer of quality content, you also can't ignore the fact that great stuff is already available. You wouldn't be working smart if you didn't allow yourself to benefit from it. The remix approach to building classroom content really is the best of both worlds.

EDUCATORS MUST UNDERSTAND COPYRIGHT AND APPROPRIATE USE. EDUCATORS MUST MODEL APPROPRIATE USE. EDUCATORS MUST TEACH APPROPRIATE USE.

· · · · · · · · · · ·

For five years, I was lucky enough to teach next door to one of my very dearest friends, Mrs. Blythe. We shared an incredible working relationship and a close friendship, so it became natural for us to share and collaborate with one another. Mrs. Blythe and I taught many of the same courses, and we agreed to have each other's backs. Our friendship and professional relationship continues to be one of the most beneficial of my career because we constantly pushed one another and supported one another, and it provided an empowering and creative space to be in.

Sometimes we created materials together and each used them with our students. Other times, we simply passed along by email a resource we found or created and encouraged the other to use it. Mrs. Blythe always ended these emails with, "Use or lose!" in the spirit of sharing—but not demanding—anyone use what she was sharing. I always appreciated this. I specifically remember one lesson Mrs. Blythe shared with me and gave me permission to use. It was light, funny, and had "Mrs. Blythe" written all over it. After looking through the activity and trying some of it, I decided to use it—without making any modifications to it because I was feeling pressed for time (total honesty, but I imagine you can relate).

We were well into the school year, and my ninth graders and I were comfortable with each other at this point. As we were going through the activity in class, one of my students said, "Mrs. Gill, you didn't make this, did you?" He had totally called me out! I jokingly insisted I did—in a way to make it clear I had not. A few other students teased me about it, and we moved on. At the time, I felt embarrassed that my students had perhaps uncovered a secret. I had taken what I convinced myself was a shortcut, and they had noticed. I took pride in creating experiences with my specific students and classroom in mind; I found myself wondering whether my students saw this "shortcut" in a negative light.

My experience of being tied to a scripted curriculum had shown me the power of creating my own instructional materials in a collective classroom voice: the voice of my students and me. This moment was pivotal because it demonstrated that students noticed a shift in the voice delivering the content. But I want to be clear: using materials you did not create is not necessarily a bad thing. If you find something amazing and feel it supports your instructional goals, find a way to use it! I share this story not to say using something "as is" will set anyone up for failure, but instead to point out that students notice your voice, too.

When you are part of the creative process, whether from the ground up or remixing, your delivery becomes more passionate, honest, and relatable. You are able to make intentional choices as you create and remix because you have a very specific audience in mind: your students. You can consider the skills you want to support in your students, their specific interests, and relevant pop culture references. You can weave your personality into your design. You can design experiences to allow you to connect with your students as a whole person. You can find ways to integrate the topics you want to address into the content you are expected to address. When teachers have the freedom to design the experiences for their class, they can tailor the materials directly to student needs. Things can be as flexible as needed to allow for reteaching, remediation, exploration, creation, or enrichment.

YOU CAN FIND WAYS TO INTEGRATE THE TOPICS YOU WANT TO ADDRESS INTO THE CONTENT YOU ARE EXPECTED TO ADDRESS.

On the other side of the coin, teachers who stick to the textbook seem to get a bad rap. But I'm not sure this is a fair assessment. Many choose to align their instruction closely with a textbook or use a scripted curriculum—even when it is not mandated of them—and it's not because they don't want to improve their instruction or do what is best for kids. Some educators choose not to exercise complete professional freedom in the classroom because of a lack of support. They aren't confident creating their own materials for any number of reasons, including a lack of planning time, not knowing where to find high-quality instructional resources, and uncertainty about how to use resources appropriately once they find them.

If you identify with the teachers I've just described, I have good news! Lots of support is available—starting with high-quality resources! Turn the page and read on!

CHAPTER 7
Resources

Although many educators are eager to embrace online resources, others may be more hesitant—either because of uncertainties mentioned previously or because of unclear messages they've received about using them. The message a district or school sends when it hopes to influence the change to online resources is critical to the success of the initiative. Even when the message and method of delivery are intentional, they will inevitably face the challenge of misunderstanding. If the message isn't specific and repeated, administrators can't expect change to happen.

Unfortunately, the increased access to technology in the classroom has brought an entire bouquet of mixed messages, one of these being educators' feelings about traditional textbooks. Let's go back to discussions schools have had about "going paperless." I have strong feelings against the use of this phrase as a technology initiative in the classroom because it has little to do with learning and supports technology initiatives in a less than thoughtful way.

If the goal is simply not to use paper, educators have forgotten their learning objectives. When they decide not to adopt textbooks any longer because they have access to more devices and a wireless Internet connection, they are on the shaky ground of making decisions based on something besides learning. If you hand your teachers an iPad and, in the same moment, announce there will no longer be a textbook adoption process, you are frustrating and confusing your teachers.

A much clearer message is sent when administrators communicate there is a better approach for their schools or districts. Making an intentional decision to refocus resources to support teachers to adopt online resources for classroom materials is a far cry from simply deciding no longer to adopt textbooks. Although a leader might intend a similar outcome in either scenario, the message sent to teachers is very different depending on how it is communicated, rolled out, reflected on, and supported. When teachers have a clear understanding of the why of adopting online resources, in addition to or in place of traditional textbooks, they are more likely to eagerly support the initiative. Luckily, moving to digital resources can happen without any sort of formal initiative at all!

OPEN EDUCATION RESOURCES

Regardless of the reason you are using digital resources (survival mode or a thoughtful decision), when first getting started in this process, you have a tendency to go to the sites you know and love already: Google, Pinterest, etc. But using platforms that were not created with educational resources and licensing in mind increases the chances of copyright violations. If you design learning experiences with copyright in mind, you must first ask yourself whether the resources you have chosen are even supposed to be used, copied, redistributed, and remixed. If you don't have permission to do all of these things, you have to rely on fair use, which can be more limiting than using openly licensed materials. If you design with copyright in mind, the first thing you will do is change the places you go to gather and curate materials you plan to use or pull from. Thankfully, there are platforms available to help you consider all of these things.

Open Educational Resources (OER) is an answer to some of the issues we have seen pop up historically as a parallel discussion to going 1:1. The US Department of Education Office of Educational Technology defines OER as "teaching, learning, and research resources that reside in the public domain or have been released under a license that permits their free use, reuse, modification, and sharing with others. Digital openly licensed resources can include complete online courses, modular digital textbooks as well as more granular resources such as images, videos, and assessment items."[1] The same office outlines the power of OER by stating that they can "increase equity, keep content relevant and high quality, empower teachers, and save money."[2] The #GoOpen movement started to bring awareness to the power these resources have to transform not only teaching but the structures educators put into place to support teaching. To read more about the #GoOpen initiative, visit tech.ed.gov. The site also shares resources, including a #GoOpen District Launch Packet to help you and your team get organized in making this shift.

Where can you go to find this buried treasure to help you work and plan smarter? When you start to explore OER, you will need to find the right resources based on your content and what works best for you and your students; therefore, I can't recommend the best for you. But I can tell you, the following are some I have found personal success with. (Just repeat after me: Pinterest is not an OER platform. Pinterest is not an OER platform.)

- Creative Commons
- OER Commons
- CK12
- Project Gutenburg
- Gooru.Org
- Amazon Inspire (Beta)

Straight to the Source of the #GoOpen Movement
-ANDREW MARCINEK-

In my effort to understand the power and the vision of the #GoOpen movement, I wanted to go straight to the source and was fortunate to spend time speaking with the person who helped get it all started: Andrew Marcinek. Andrew, currently the Chief Information Office at Worcester Academy in Massachusetts, was the Chief Open Education Advisor for the US Department of Education Office of Educational Technology, and he launched the #GoOpen movement in October of 2015 during the Obama administration. Andrew was brought on as the first Advisor, a role springing out of the president's ConnectEd Plan, which focused on creating accessibility and equality of educational resources. His specific work was to engage educators to look at open educational resources.

Andrew explained that his role "grew out of ConnectED, which was put forth by the Obama White House and was designed to support equitable access to mobile devices, technology resources, high-quality teacher training within these realms, high-speed broadband, etc. The goal was to provide access to shareable and modifiable educational materials. This fourth tenet was essentially one of the things I was working to move forward. We launched the movement and energized a group of people to be the pathfinders and trailblazers. While I was there, I ran a large-scale campaign to garner excitement, generate proof points, and provide resources so people could understand what all of this is about."

Given Andrew's work in this field, I asked him two specific questions. First, how can educators, new to OER, understand how it can help them? Second, how do schools get started in supporting teachers in using Open Education Resources when they often see only hurdles? "In relation to the second question, I have seen a broad spectrum of how using these resources is being approached in schools. On the extreme end of the spectrum—where schools are perhaps overly eager to embrace OER—I've seen schools hand teachers and students a device, declare they are no longer adopting textbooks, and let everyone just go for it!"

As Andrew reflected on this situation when it was occurring a decade ago, he said, "A leader made a decision to try an OER initiative, but things quickly scattered. Things quickly got out of hand back then and remained so for years.

"I like to use streaming music as an example of this. In an ideal world, I would love to have the business model of Spotify and blend it with Yelp, and this model would be how we purchase education materials. If everyone could spend a set amount per year on educational materials—open and vetted by individual, trusted, and verified reviews from all over the country—you would have the perfect system.

"What is preventing us from doing this? One of many reasons is that there is no central repository. Some people love Spotify, some Apple Music, or whatever else is out there.

"OER is still difficult because there are many different resource hubs you can go to. Some are better than others, but it is a tricky space to get into. You have to start with your why and organize a team of thinkers from all different stakeholders. You have to figure out what is going to work best for you to make it work."

In response to where to start, Andrew guides by sharing, "I think it is first developing a why. It really doesn't take that much time, but it takes tremendous organization. This isn't about convincing everyone that textbooks are bad: that was never the goal. But thinking about what textbooks cost—what if we took all of that money and reinvested it in our teachers? What if we were able to provide professional development so that teachers can learn how to do this and build critical mass within a district or within a school to drive that change?"

Andrew also identified a fringe benefit to supporting teachers from an organic level. Not only does this help encourage educators to explore the world of OER, but it also helps develop teacher leaders. In turn, this can initiate action and drive the movement forward. Above all, Andrew stressed the importance of understanding the why behind a school choosing to adopt Open Educational Resources instead of traditional textbooks. He shared that some of the most successful school districts are those turning to Open Educational Resources based on student-centered decision-making rather than basing the decision on the financial piece. These districts understand that with a traditional textbook adoption they might have to wait years for materials to get updated, but using OER allows them to revisit the relevance of their materials consistently.

As Andrew concluded, "Ultimately, this idea is reinvesting in the profession of teaching—giving teachers creative license and control. It is professionalizing the teaching profession. We are no longer taking scripts essentially produced by only three companies and vetted by two large state consortiums. OER gives school districts local control of their resources. You don't have to wait for six or seven years for new curricula to come out. You can revise it every year as the times change. It creates more autonomy. It might create more work, but it pushes educators to be better."

THE MYTH OF FAIR USE

Many assume that if a resource is free, it is also available for use by educators; however, the cost of something and its copyright and licensing are not necessarily related. A resource can be free and locked down while another item might require payment but be completely openly licensed. Open Educational Resources are not synonymous with "free of cost" resources.

The most important takeaway in support of responsible creation is to acknowledge that educational use does not guarantee permission for you to use whatever you'd like to use in whatever way you'd like to use it. All too often, educators simply slap onto their planning practices the phrase "educational use" and assume they've done enough. This misconception runs rampant through school hallways—like students on their way to the cafeteria on chicken nugget day.

Educational use does not guarantee educators the right to retain, remix, copy, or distribute materials in class.

Fair use is a defense allowing people to use copyrighted materials for teaching, reporting, parody, research, and criticism. But this defense holds only if the users weigh the four factors of fair use when making our decisions on what and how to implement a resource. Essentially, these factors are an approach to using copyrighted material without special permission—and all of them must be considered. As an analogy, they keep your boat floating. If you can't afford to take on any water, throwing one of them (the factors) overboard won't help! You must weigh all four factors when you make a choice about what you are using and how you are using it in your classroom. These four factors are the guidelines to ensure that the way you are using something for your classrooms truly is within fair use.

In an effort to provide clarity, educators hope to find a magic bullet—a list outlining what they can and can't do. You have likely asked questions like the following:

- What percentage of a written work can I use?
- Am I safe if I use just thirty seconds of a song?
- Are video clips safe to use as long as I only use two-minute segments?

SIMPLY CALLING SOMETHING "EDUCATIONAL USE" DOES NOT MAKE YOU COPYRIGHT COMPLIANT.

Confession time: I used to ask these same questions. In fact, at some point in my career, I'm sure I've made every mistake I am outlining in this book. Simply calling something "educational use" does not make you copyright compliant. And no "magic number of seconds" of a song or "percentage of a work" ensures your purpose will fall under fair use. Educators can use copyrighted material, but they must be considerate of a few things. In fact, these considerations help you do better and plan better. Understanding fair use and applying it with fidelity is the foundation for a classroom celebrating copyright and the protection of intellectual property.

THE FOUR FACTORS[3]

FACTOR ONE: PURPOSE AND CHARACTER OF USE

Focus on the how! Think about your goals and the way you are using the copyrighted materials. Factor one supports using copyrighted materials for instructional and transformative use. The US Copyright Office defines transformative uses as "those that add something new, with a further purpose of different character, and do not substitute for the original use of the work." EDUspeak says, "Use the material as part of direct instruction or to create something new."

FACTOR TWO: NATURE OF THE WORK

Focus on the *what!* When you look at factor two, you must consider the overall goal of copyright itself. Copyright aims to protect works of creative expression. As a general rule, the more creative the work is, the less likely your use can be considered fair.

The US Copyright Office defines this factor as "the degree to which the work that was used relates to the copyright's purpose of encouraging creative expression. Thus, using a more creative or imaginative work (such as a novel, movie, or song) is less likely to support a claim of fair use than using a factual work (such as a technical article or news item). In addition, use of an unpublished work is less likely to be considered fair." In EDUspeak, this factor asks, "What is the original purpose of the work?"

FACTOR THREE: PORTION USED IN RELATION TO THE WHOLE

Focus on the size! This factor helps you determine what excerpts, sections, or clips you should be using to meet your goals. Remember, there aren't any percentages or time regulations you can follow to make this simple. Instead, approach this on a case-by-case basis and make decisions driven by content.

Again, the misconception is in thinking a magical list of numbers exists to help you with this factor. For example, I have heard many educators assume they are safe if they only use thirty seconds of a song. (Say it with me: No numbers exist! NO NUMBERS EXIST!) In general, using a small part of the work over using a large portion of the work is more likely to be determined fair use. But this is not always true. In some cases, using an entire work has been considered fair use, whereas in other cases, using a small paragraph has not been found to be fair use. You have to use your best judgment. The question to ask yourself is, "What is the smallest amount I can use to achieve the instructional and learning goal?"

The US Copyright Office states, "Under this factor, courts look at both the quantity and quality of the work." EDUspeak says, "Use the smallest amount necessary to achieve your instructional goals."

THERE AREN'T ANY PERCENTAGES OR TIME REGULATIONS YOU CAN FOLLOW TO MAKE THIS SIMPLE. INSTEAD, APPROACH THIS ON A CASE-BY-CASE BASIS AND MAKE DECISIONS DRIVEN BY CONTENT.

· · · · · · · · · · ·

FACTOR FOUR: EFFECT ON POTENTIAL VALUE

Focus on how your use of the content in your class might impact any potential sale(s) for the copyright holder. Your use should have no impact on this. Although it seems easy for educators to simply justify their use of any materials as "educational," they must consider the copyright holder and whether they may be harming potential sales for the creator. When determining whether your specific instance falls under fair use, ask yourself whether your use would cause the copyright holder to lose money or a possible sale.

According to the US Copyright Office definition, "Here, courts review whether, and to what extent, the unlicensed use harms the existing or future market for the copyright owner's original work." EDUspeak says, "Don't get in the way of a potential sale."

If you feel you aren't standing on solid ground after reading about the four factors, don't fear! You are completely normal. The four factors live in—and feed off of—the gray area. Every case has to be looked at on an individual basis. It isn't a perfect science, but you can feel good knowing you are doing the very best you can when you consider the four factors when making decisions. You now have a few questions to keep in the back of your mind when you are remixing:

· What are my goals for my students?

· What materials will support reaching these goals?

- Am I using these materials in a way that protects creative and intellectual property?
- How can I remix and package this in a way that reaches my students?

Having an understanding of fair use can help you answer all of these questions and be more thoughtful about the instructional choices you make. When you are using works in a transformational way or for close reading, your instruction improves as you become more intentional about the use of supplemental materials. When you are confident in how you can use, modify, and distribute instructional materials, remixing them can add authentic teacher voice (helping you avoid getting called out by your students!). Instead of looking at copyright and fair use as restrictions to what you do every day—or as the death of creativity—shift your mindset to be open about how copyright can actually elevate what you do.

THE PUBLIC DOMAIN

Educators can search for materials to use and remix for their classrooms in a number of ways that do not require them to think much about the four factors of fair use or copyright at all. One of these avenues is to consider items within the public domain. The public domain is a jackpot of resources for creators. According to the US Copyright Office:

> The public domain is not a place. A work of authorship is in the "public domain" if it is no longer under copyright protection or if it failed to meet the requirements for copyright protection. Works in the public domain may be used freely without the permission of the former copyright owner.[4]

Current copyright law protects works created after 1978 for the life of the author plus seventy years.[5] But of course, as with any topic related to copyright, duration is complicated and depends on a number of factors. You can read about them all on the US Copyright Office website.

Films, literature, and images that live in the public domain provide us with a buffet of items we can use however we want. Using items from the public domain does not require attribution of any kind. Work smarter, am I right? I feel as though it almost becomes a game in which you earn extra points for yourself if you locate something that you want to use and it is either licensed CC0 (Creative Commons = no rights reserved) or is within the public domain. What do you win? The freedom of skipping the step of attribution, of course!

As I wrote this book, "Public Domain Day" was celebrated. This occurs on January 1 and is the day previously protected works enter the public domain. Copyright protection lasts for the duration of the author's life plus seventy years; however, the protection ends at the end of the seventieth year. As such, all works entering the public domain do so on January 1. Public Domain Day this year (2019) was especially significant because the works published in 1923 were the first ones protected under the Sonny Bono Copyright Extension Act, giving them the seventy years of protection, twenty more than the fifty years of protection given to works published the year before.

If you are searching for any type of media to enrich your content, finding a work within the public domain gives you complete and total freedom to use it in a powerful way without worrying about copyright at all. But even though you won't have to "worry" about it, you have another great opportunity to chat with your students about how copyright law has changed and what it protects.

CHAPTER 8
Building the Creator in You
(Voice Lessons)

As you begin to navigate OER and public domain content, you may become overwhelmed by the volume of resources available. You will find it necessary to acquire or hone some skills to discern the best resources for your class's unique needs.

SKILLS OF THE OER CURATOR AND CREATOR

BECOME A CURATOR

Forget about Pinterest for a second. I know, I know! Pinterest is great for recipes, but probably not for finding high-quality, openly licensed resources. Use the right tool for the job, and save yourself time and energy by shifting toward platforms that make it easier for you to locate high-quality materials. Become familiar with OER platforms, find your favorites, and turn those into your "go-to's."

TRAIN YOUR EYE TO NOTICE HIGH QUALITY

Why is it easier to absorb chunked content? Why is it easier to read certain colors and texts on a device than others? (H/T to Michele Eaton for first bringing these items to my attention.) What types of questions are being asked within the content? Are activities asking students to learn actively and create? These are questions you want to keep in mind as you're reviewing online content. Read up on proactive accessibility. Think about how content interacts with the devices your students have available to them. Think about the login process. Beyond knowing where to go to find high-quality content and tools, also know what you aren't willing to sacrifice in your content.

LEARN TO VET CONTENT

Schools tend to overlook providing PD for teachers to work together and agree on a process for vetting content. Vetting doesn't always need to be a formal process, but it is powerful to have conversations about it and understand what "high quality" means when applied to content. What qualities are priority to look for in content? Whether you work as a team to create a vetting rubric for adopting resources more formally or you work independently to curate resources, having a clear vision of high-quality content ensures your success when making decisions about what resources to use. With practice, vetting for high-quality content eventually becomes instinctual.

PLAN SMARTER

Plan smarter by knowing when you need to create from scratch, when you can remix, or when you can use something as it exists. Rethink what "planning" even means. Create platforms for your students to experience learning rather than creating or collecting content for them to consume. When you begin to think of your students as creators and explorers, your planning will start to shift. Curate tools for your students to create with instead of putting the pressure of creation only on yourself.

RESPOND TO FEEDBACK FROM STUDENTS

How often do you ask your students to give feedback on the learning in your classroom? You expect your students to be comfortable with receiving feedback on a daily basis, but do you show them how to give feedback? Do you help them understand how to give helpful feedback? Set norms that provide opportunities for feedback to be two-way: between your students and you. Create a system to ask how you can make learning better in your classroom. When you try something new in your classroom, consider creating a simple Google Form or another way to collect feedback from your students. Ask them how they felt about their learning experience. Not only will this give you insight from your students' perspectives, but it will also help build (or reinforce) your relationship with them and an environment of trust.

GET EYES ON YOUR WORK

Ask people to review your work, seeking out those you know will be honest with you. Ask people outside your content area, within your content area, or even someone who isn't an educator. Ask a student aide for feedback or share on Twitter and ask for responses. Find your trusted group and return the favor for them as well. If these people—who aren't students in your classroom—can navigate your content, take it as a sign that your work is well organized and clear to users.

RESPOND TO CONSTRUCTIVE CRITICISM—LIKE A PRO

Purposefully building this skill took me a while. It didn't feel great to have people pointing out my flaws. Creation can be deeply personal, and having flaws pointed out can sting at times—we are human. When you create (and educators are all creators!), you perhaps make yourself more vulnerable than when you do anything else. When you reveal yourself through the work you create, you will get criticism. This is absolutely inevitable. Instead of fighting the criticism, I suggest you become friends with it. In fact, become so comfortable receiving feedback and constructive criticism, you let it fuel you.

CREATE PLATFORMS FOR YOUR STUDENTS TO EXPERIENCE LEARNING RATHER THAN CREATING OR COLLECTING CONTENT FOR THEM TO CONSUME.

· · · · · · · · · · ·

Responding intelligently to true constructive criticism can make you an all-around better educator (even a better person). If you have a growth mindset, you want to get better, and constructive criticism is an effective tool to leverage when you want to grow. When you react positively to constructive criticism, you show you value the time your coworkers took to give you feedback, you value what they say, and you listen to them. This skill is powerful in all school relationships: teacher to student, teacher to administrator, teacher to teacher—even teacher to parent. Learn to listen, not make excuses, and say thank you. Then visibly respond to feedback by making changes. When others watch you through the process, they will see that you are open to learning from others, and they will be more willing to provide feedback in the future.

This is also cyclical. When you show others how leaders (all educators are leaders) respond to feedback, they will take your constructive feedback of them more seriously because you have already demonstrated you can accept theirs.

CREATE ITEMS TO FILL GAPS

One of the main reasons I became motivated to create my own materials was that I found myself in serious need of materials to address skills my students needed to master. I was charged with supporting them through the process, and tons of materials were available, but none of them were curated in such a way as to help me from start to finish. Following a textbook from cover to cover wasn't something I ever did. A novel I was reading with my students would inspire me to create a project-based experience for them, for example. And while I found myself really loving that part of my job, I wasn't always intentional about knowing why I was making the decisions I was making, knowing how to vet the content I was using, or knowing how to responsibly create with copyright in mind.

During my interview for my role as an instructional technology coach, I was asked to tell about something I had created that didn't already exist. I had recently wrapped up Romeo and Juliet (most of my favorite memories as a classroom teacher are related to this play!) and, even though I wasn't sure how well my answer would be received, I had to answer with what had organically come to mind. My students had created dating app profiles for different characters in the play. I had created a template, with the students using Google Drawings so we could create our dating "app," and each decision they made in the app had to be backed by textual evidence and lines specifically related to characterization.

This interview question asked me to draw specifically on my experience in creating something new for students to use, and that provided evidence that creation was encouraged and expected. As you begin working with online content, start by looking for the gaps you see in your current resources. If you can't fill those gaps with the supplemental resources you find, use this as motivation to create something you are wanting. What better way to stay focused on student learning objectives as you design!?

Even though countless resources are available, I'll argue that you will never find any single resource—or even curate a collection of resources—that would be unable to benefit from something supplemental, something to fill a gap, or something that can respond to current trends and interests.

TRUST YOU KNOW WHAT YOUR STUDENTSNEED

Educators constantly collect all types of data. Use the data in your planning process to inform the choices you make about digital content, direct instruction, differentiation, etc. Through the relationships you build, the evidence you collect, and the conclusions you draw, you are the one best suited to design in a way that works for your students currently in your room.

WORK SMARTER—INVOLVE YOUR STUDENTS

In my early educator life, I believed I had to work my tail off all of the time for my lessons to be successful. Let me be clear: I am not suggesting teachers don't work hard, because they do. In fact, in my opinion, "work hard and be nice to people" is a perfect mantra for life. I am suggesting, though, that you rethink your definition of "working hard" to elevate your practice into one focusing on student learning and student creation.

Before a new literature unit, I often created a presentation to give my students some essential background information about the author, the historical significance of the literary work, or the themes we would be discussing. I created a dynamic slideshow presentation or a nausea-inducing Prezi. I would cram into the thing every piece of information I could about Steinbeck or Shakespeare, including what I thought were fun images and engaging memes. Then I showed up ready to throw all the information at my students. What was I doing!? Who had done all of the work? Me! What did my students learn from all my work? Only how much I knew about Shakespeare.

Creating a learning experience doesn't mean you have to work yourself to death and lose sleep perfecting every little detail. Shift your thinking to create materials to allow your students to do the learning. I could have saved myself a lot of heartache, late nights, and anxious planning if I had learned this lesson much sooner.

PART THREE:
REVERSE

=

Share Everything

CHAPTER 9
An Attitude of Sharing

About four years ago at an Indiana Summer of eLearning conference in Warsaw, Indiana, I was presenting a session called "Build a Blog," during which I shared ideas on how to get started with student blogging and suggestions on giving feedback. I had been a technology coach for only about a year and was still building my confidence as a presenter. On the second day of the conference, I walked into my presenter room and found a note written on the dry erase board: "Diana, I sent you a message on Twitter. Come find me in room 123." I checked my Twitter messages and saw a message from Matt Miller, author of Ditch That Textbook, saying he had a crazy idea.

I practically sprinted to his room—he is an author/educator I had looked up to for some time! Matt had noticed he was scheduled to give a session on blogging at the exact time of my blogging session, and he asked whether I wanted to team up and present together. (Um, yes! How gracious and thoughtful of a dude is he?!) During our session, I shared and gave access to my presentation materials and encouraged participants to use the materials, saying, "These are yours to use; I don't even need credit." Matt responded with, "Wow, that's really generous!"

SHARE EVERYTHING

Collaborating with Matt on the fly was definitely an exciting experience, and I left reflecting on my practice of sharing and Matt's comment. As a teacher, I had never considered not sharing. When I was a preservice teacher, one of my undergrad friends had given me a creative idea for an activity. When I told him I had used it in one of my field experiences—giving him total credit for it—he said, "Diana, I don't need credit. Use it! Take the credit!" My conversation with him solidified for me the attitude of sharing everything.

Educators absolutely need to help each other out. I don't believe that sharing the materials I create and curate is overly generous or sacrificial, because I know the educators I share with will reciprocate. They will be just as happy to share with me when they create something they are excited about or when I am looking for help. (There is another side to this, and I'm not suggesting we rip each other off, ever.)

Honestly, not a day goes by when I don't reach out to someone in my PLN. If I am looking for a hyperdoc on a topic, I'll head to #hyperdocs on Twitter or the hyperdoc Facebook group page. If I need training materials, I reach out to fellow Google trainers I know. My Google Innovator group (WDC17!) is active every day in our group Google Hangout. It's a constant thread of thirty-plus people asking for advice, ideas, and resources. Sharing resources is just one of the many benefits of a PLN. The amazing and generous educators I surround myself with—both virtually and in person—are one hundred percent of the reason I can keep my head up through the hard times. I look to them for motivation and to challenge myself. Sometimes I look to them for reassurance. I've been very intentional about giving back to these groups. It's all about the sharing.

Sometimes, sharing means you have less of something that you had originally. For example, if I have an entire pizza and I share some of it, now I only get to eat a portion instead of the whole thing. (Don't judge me! I really love pizza!) However, when you share in education, you don't lose anything. Instead, you gain connections. You gain feedback. You gain a group of like-minded educators who care about the same things you care about and help you continue to grow. When you share, you ultimately have more in the end.

BUILDING A PERSONAL LEARNING NETWORK

How can you build a PLN or expand the one you already have? A PLN is made up of the relationships you build with other educators. This network can be a huge support and resource to you. Think about the people who make up your PLN; consider dedicating some energy to expanding your network. Connected educators know you can never have enough connections.

Start by connecting with educators in the same role as you. Find someone in your building, in another building within your district, in a neighboring district, or across your state. Ask this person to be a sounding board for you—someone you can bounce ideas off of, vent to, and celebrate successes with. Start with an email or a Google Hangout chat. Ask if you can come visit a classroom. I've found that administrators usually support finding coverage for your classroom if you request to observe another teacher!

Find a mentor. If your district does not have a formal mentorship program, create a mentor for yourself. It might be a veteran teacher you can seek advice from, an approachable administrator, or a friend working in another state that you connect with on Facebook.

FIND A MENTOR. IF YOUR DISTRICT DOES NOT HAVE A FORMAL MENTORSHIP PROGRAM, CREATE A MENTOR FOR YOURSELF.

· · · · · · · · · · ·

Get into the virtual spaces. Get on Twitter. If this intimidates you, find a Twitterati in your school and ask for help. (Trust me, they will help you!) Follow authors of books and blogs you've read. Jump on Google Plus Communities. Every state has a Google Educator Group (GEG), and this is a great way to get started. You can search for communities supporting educators within your subject area or passion. Be open to trying new ways to connect, too. I've found Voxer and Marco Polo are great platforms to host your deeper discussions. My very closest friend and educator group uses Marco Polo to stay connected, and to engage in the occasional educational debate. If all of these apps and tools intimidate you, choose just one at first and jump in.

Connect with educators who have similar interests. These connections will happen naturally as you continue to find platforms. Twitter chats and hashtags are great for this. Find the people who are talking about what you want to talk about and join in. Connect with people in your community who are working in the field. Connect them with your students. Look for ways they can support the work you are doing. The longer I am in the amazing field of education, the more I learn about the power of simply asking, and I find that the world is a very generous place.

The first-year teacher, truly in survival mode, might rely on you to guide them. Maybe something you share will be eye opening for a teacher who has been looking to try something new but is lost. An engaging activity you share could inspire a teacher to reinvent her classroom after the experience gets students fired up about learning. Maybe you aren't ready to share just yet, but you are looking forward to building your creative skills so you can give back to other educators who have shared so much with you. Teaching is hard. Very hard. Sharing with others is one thing you can do to say, "Hey, I have your back."

CHAPTER 10
The Challenges of Sharing

Sometimes sharing what you work so hard to create is challenging. These challenges can be difficult to overcome; in fact, at times they make me hesitant to share. Teachers have confided in me that they don't always feel like the sharing is reciprocated. Maybe the work you get back isn't as high quality as you would like. Sharing can also make you feel vulnerable. What if someone judges your work? Maybe someone has used something you are really proud of without giving you credit. Or even worse, perhaps you have been a victim of someone using your material and personally making money from it. These are all very real issues, and they need to be explored—to determine how they can be overcome.

WHY EDUCATORS DON'T ALWAYS WANT TO SHARE

MY MATERIALS AREN'T GOOD ENOUGH

Not everything educators do in their classrooms is a home run. I remember one situation in particular when I basically struck out. I was still living in the stressed-out and awful "get to everything on the map" mentality; I quickly threw together an activity I knew wasn't my best work, but I felt I needed to cover a concept on the list. We did the activity as a mini lesson at the start of class, and during the lesson, I noticed one of my normally more engaged students was not connected and seemed spacey. Later, I asked the student. "Hey, what did you think of the lesson? Did it help you understand the concept? I noticed you didn't seem to love it." The response I got didn't surprise me at all: "Honestly, Mrs. Gill, you have had better stuff."

I knew before I began the lesson execution that it wasn't going to be a home run. As such, I shouldn't have used it in the first place. But this story highlights a few things: One, educators are all stressed for time, so they can allow themselves a certain amount of grace because of this. Two, educators know when their material is good—and when it isn't. Would I have been eager to share this activity with other teachers? Probably not. But maybe I should have asked for feedback. Maybe I should have reached out to others to see whether they were willing to share an awesome activity to cover the needed skill.

Educators must get into the habit of sharing the content they are proud of. If you are honest with yourself, when you create something good, you know it. And your good can become even better when you share. Maybe your cool idea is missing something, but a trusted colleague might be able to make it even better. The key is being willing to take the leap and share.

A few years ago, I brainstormed an activity for students involving Play-doh and a lot of symbolism. It was to be done collaboratively at the conclusion of reading a short story. I was excited about it, and I shared it with a friend. She evaluated it but ultimately decided not to do it. Perhaps she wanted to go in a different direction, was looking for something more concrete, or simply wanted to spend her time with students in a different way. My feelings weren't hurt by her decision, but, as I consider this story years later, I realize that if I had asked her why she didn't see my idea playing out in her room, I may have discovered a way to improve the lesson. Second, she saw that the activity wasn't for her, and she felt comfortable moving on. This is a professional creative freedom we have to allow educators.

OTHERS WILL CRITICIZE ME

As I said earlier, when you are creative, you will receive criticism from someone. The good news is you get to choose what you do with it! I was criticized by someone who thought I just "had fun" in my classroom. This got under my skin, and it took me a while to think through it clearly. This person did not take me seriously, and I was mad—really mad. A bunch of questions ran through my mind:

- How does he know what I am doing in my classroom?
- Is this related to age difference?

- What is so bad about having fun?
- Do they not think my students are learning?

Likely, most educators can think of a peer who has unnecessarily or unjustifiably criticized them. Even if you can rationalize through it and you don't think those negative things about yourself, the criticism can still sting.

I developed a strategy to put things into perspective. Each day I asked myself, "Do you feel good about what you did today?" If I could answer yes, I was proud of what I had done. And I don't mean I had the perfect lesson or I killed it! But did I put in the effort my students deserve? If you can answer yes to this question, then let the critics talk. They will always be around, and you may never change their minds about you. But you don't have to let them discourage your creativity. In fact, their reaction to what you are doing is more about them than it is about you.

OTHERS DON'T SHARE IN RETURN

I have been on both sides of this. As a classroom teacher, I was in situations where I felt I was taking much more than I was giving. In other situations, I was the one who was giving all I was creating but getting nothing in return. I didn't mind sharing because I knew what it felt like to rely on support from others. But you wouldn't be human if you didn't have this thought cross your mind: Wait—I'm doing a lot of the work here. While sharing might be harder to justify in this situation, I don't accept this as a valid reason to stop sharing. Instead, I see this as an opportunity to build a strong culture of sharing by modeling that altruism doesn't come with an I.O.U.

SHARING IMPLIES THE NEED TO IMPROVE

Some educators believe that if they volunteer to share, their offer equates to stating an underlying idea that someone else needs to improve. Guess what? Educators should always seek to improve. And all educators can improve. This is central to embracing a growth mindset. If someone shares with me or offers to support me in any way, I can't assume their motivation was to suggest I wasn't doing a good enough job. This is silly. Seeing the work of others, even if you decide not to use it, makes your own work better. You might learn a different strategy you can apply to another situation. Peer review and coaching of any type can only be helpful if you are truly open to growth.

THE FREEDOM OF "FREE"

Recently, I had a conversation with a teacher reminding me why this message is so important. We were originally discussing how to create an interactive activity similar to items she had seen on Pinterest. "Diana, I keep finding things I can buy online that I want to use, but I'm out of money." Her honest sharing of this is so central to the mission of Copyrighteous, and I felt an overwhelming responsibility to support her and use this opportunity to empower her to never again to spend a dime on something she could find or create herself.

I completely understand why educators might turn to a paid platform to find content. Educators are under huge pressure to perform and produce. However, how can educators—who are often put in the position of having to spend their own money on simple classroom materials such as paper and pens—be expected to pay for materials to support the curriculum as well? Recently, a teacher showed me a presentation she purchased on Teachers Pay Teachers for twenty dollars. Twenty dollars! For one PowerPoint! I understand why educators might choose to sell items online, but consider who is purchasing the content. Asking a teacher to spend part of his or her own salary on something I can simply share doesn't sit right with me. And I don't feel taken advantage of when I share, because I know my network will return the favor and share something to help me. Again, the relationship is built on sharing.

The practice of teachers selling items online is also complicated by ownership questions. Who truly owns teacher-created materials? The short answer: probably your district. If you create materials as part of your employment, or as a work for hire, your employer owns these resources. If teacher materials are created during school hours, on school property, using school resources, and are within the scope of your employment, they are technically owned by the district. Even if nothing is explicitly written in your contract about this, work for hire applies. (This is a conversation worth having with your district leadership team.)

After working with the teacher I previously mentioned for about twenty minutes, we had created the start of something to use with her students that she was really excited about—and she didn't have to spend any money! We didn't do anything crazy or magical; we simply took time to have a conversation about what she wanted students to be able to do and then used our resources to support this goal. Before our conversation, I don't think she recognized that she already had the skills needed to build this activity for her students. She was excited to share it with the rest of her grade-level team. The staff of another building in our district heard about the idea and reached out to learn more about it so they too could create their own version of it. This is the magic educators find through sharing.

BEG, BORROW, AND BUY?

Teachers Pay Teachers is a platform claiming to be the most popular place for teachers to find materials for their classrooms, citing five million educators using the site in 2017 alone. With over three million resources available to purchase and download, it makes sense that teachers would gravitate toward its potential. Teachers have told me that Teachers Pay Teachers is their "go to." Teachers all over the country are using this site to make their materials available to other educators—most likely with a price tag and strict rules about usage attached. Wouldn't this be an amazing concept if all of the resources were free and openly licensed?

When I reflect on my position on Teachers Pay Teachers, Fiverr comes to mind. Fiverr is a popular platform allowing you to connect with freelance creators and hire them to do projects for you such as write a jingle for your podcast, create a logo for your side hustle, draw a caricature for your Twitter profile pic, etc. While I had initially wondered whether the goal of Fiverr ran parallel to the goal of Teachers Pay Teachers, I realized the largest difference is the audience and market of each site. Fiverr's customers are not creators; they are purchasing content from creators. Likely the producers and consumers are not from the same profession. In contrast, the consumers of Teachers Pay Teachers...are teachers! The producers and consumers are of the same cloth.

Fiverr offers a product I really might not be capable of creating. Maybe I could learn to play the piano and learn to compose to write the catchiest jingle of all time. But music and marketing are not my chosen profession. Education is. I do know what my students need. I do know how to deliver content in a way to reach my students. I do understand the intricacies of laying something out in a way to connect one concept to another. As an educator, I can design content. Educators know how to do all of these things—and more. Why aren't they harnessing all of their passion and power? Why are they letting others tell them the best way to deliver content to students? What aren't we doing to make sure teachers feel like they have the support to do these things? Teachers Pay Teachers sends the message that not all educators can and should create for our students. In reality, all educators can build the skills they need to create for their students.

Assuming that people are inherently good and operate with positive intentions (I like to believe this because it keeps me sane!), I want to consider how Teachers Pay Teachers can be an opportunity to help teachers get started with creating and remixing their own instructional materials. Teachers Pay Teachers requires sellers to provide their first resource for free. These teachers do not possess magical skills others can't grow and build on. The fact that so many educators use Teachers Pay Teachers might actually be a good sign. It means they want to find the best materials for their students. It means they have already "ditched the textbook" and are looking to get out of the box, break the rules, and dump the scripted curriculum. It means they are looking for better ideas or resources than they feel they currently have. It means they have evaluated what they have done in the past and are looking to mix it up. Thankfully, it also means many teachers are proud to share their work and recognize that others can benefit from it. And while I am giving the process the benefit of the doubt, I hope that educators are hungry for a better way.

WHAT WOULD HAPPEN IF SCHOOLS INVESTED IN THEIR OWN TEACHERS?

Teachers Pay Teachers also has an option for schools and districts to have an account, allowing teachers to request items to be purchased under this account. The administrator account can approve or deny these requests and, if the item is approved, the district pays for the resource. While I appreciate districts taking financial responsibility off of individual teachers in this scenario, I still believe it sends a message to teachers that they aren't capable of creating personally. This is a missed opportunity for schools and districts to empower teachers. What would happen if schools invested in their own teachers? What if they empowered their teachers to create content specific to their students by carving out time and resources to support them in doing so?

School administration has the responsibility to build capacity for teachers. Purchasing an account to build an online library of instructional materials from Teachers Pay Teachers is the same as purchasing a textbook.

Moving our textbook dollars to Teachers Pay Teachers isn't revolutionary and isn't helping teachers gain skills personally. Educators can buy an entire year of curriculum on Teachers Pay Teachers to be used in their classes. For example, for five hundred dollars, you can purchase an algebra curriculum for an entire year, and it includes 740 pages of resources. This curriculum is licensed to allow only one teacher to use the resources. While the license allows the teacher to make some modifications, such as test question edits, the materials aren't openly licensed.

Many of the resources available on the site are completely locked PDFs that do not allow teachers to make modifications at all. For example, a digital download for a graphic organizer, including an answer key, has a low price of two dollars, but it is in PDF form. Depending on what type of device your students have, the file type of the resource might seriously limit the potential for delivery options and opportunities for blended instruction. It would be preferable if this were delivered in a form in which a teacher could make modifications to it to maximize its student reach. Better yet is for educators to help each other recognize the opportunity for student creation when it presents itself. Organizing ideas from reading into a graphic is a perfect example but, instead of purchasing a graphic organizer to print and ask your students to complete, why not ask students to sketchnote, create an infographic on Canva or Google Slides, create a mind map on Google Drawings, or make an interactive multimedia text set on Thinglink instead? I challenge you to recognize your own ability to know your students and your content, recognize high-quality materials when you see them, and explore new ways to curate the dynamic curriculum you are looking to deliver.

As I mentioned previously, the first step in building these skills directs us to a new world with new rules: planet OER. There you will find what you need, not only to build your skills, but in some cases also to gain access to previously vetted material—something Teachers Pay Teachers and Pinterest don't offer. (Vetting and reviews are not created equal.) As you think about the topics in your class—maybe one you aren't confident in—you may decide you need to draw from another's perspective rather than create items from scratch. But Teachers Pay Teachers and Pinterest shouldn't be the places you turn to for materials to put in front of your students. You need to be absolutely certain the material they have access to is high quality, unbiased, historically accurate, etc. You must shift your practice so the materials you curate or adopt to use with students go through two layers of vetting.

First, the vendor, website, or organization should provide vetting as part of their requirements for making items available. Teachers Pay Teachers and Pinterest do not vet the materials on their sites. Second, and even more important, you must add vetting into your process when you plan learning experiences for your students. Even if platforms do have a dedicated staff of educators vetting the resources being made publicly available, the conversations you have at the classroom level are more powerful. Just like you can't assume other drivers on the road will make decisions to keep you safe, you can't assume anything online is ready to be put into the hands of our students. You need to plan defensively. And no matter how deliberate or subconscious your personal process of vetting content currently is, copyright, fair use, and responsible use should be the foundation of your process. Likely, you'd never steal a car—don't drive stolen content either!

VETTING

I've debated the use of Teachers Pay Teachers with dozens of educators. In an episode of the 411 Vodcast, a vodcast project I work on with a few friends, we had a healthy debate about it. In fact, for well over a year before this specific episode, we debated whether we would even record an episode on the topic. Chris Young, one of the members of the group who is largely neutral on the Teachers Pay Teachers topic, said the best argument against it is the vetting argument. I have seen threads on Twitter in which educators are calling out other educators for poor-quality or offensive content found on the site. And while I know everything on Teachers Pay Teachers will not be high quality, their lack of vetting is low on my list of reasons I don't support their model. OER isn't a perfect process when it comes to vetting, either. In fact, searching hashtags on Twitter or finding any platform sharing openly licensed material or teacher-created content won't be a perfect process either. Certainly searching for vetted and reviewed materials saves educators time, but it is still important that they internalize a process for vetting their own content. This is a major component of information literacy. You need personal metrics to use to decide whether something is relevant, high quality, and credible.

I'll argue that educators don't necessarily need to have a formalized process for vetting, but instead need to go through the process of evaluating what vetting values. Initially, you might not be able to identify high-quality resources, especially when it comes to digital content. Something as simple as color choices can impact the functionality of an activity you create for students. This is largely one of those "you don't know what you don't know" situations and was something I didn't learn until I was a few years into my role in edtech. Vetting content is an essential teacher skill often overlooked when educators create a PD plan. And simply because you have a teaching license doesn't mean you know how to identify high-quality materials. But the good news is that we can learn.

The mark of a growth mindset is believing you are not perfect and looking at everything as an opportunity to grow. If you use materials without fully vetting them, reflect on this and ask yourself, "What would I do differently next time?" Thoughtfully consider what might benefit from improvements, or have conversations with other teachers in your building about what high-quality digital content must have. Ask questions such as:

- What would cause something immediately to be considered not high quality?
- How does accessibility play into this?
- What qualities are mandatory? Preferred?
- What are your non-negotiables when you choose content?

Work with your team to find the right answers to these questions, and then apply what you learn to the new materials you create.

State Education Technology Directors Association (SETDA) is an excellent resource to find information to help you learn how to vet content. (https://qualitycontent.setda.org/oer/vetting-oer/)

CHAPTER 11 ○
Tackling the Challenges of Sharing

Clearly, sharing teacher-created instructional materials doesn't always happen naturally. In fact, as I just mentioned, educators can spend a lot of time talking about why they shouldn't share, and likely you can add some additional reasons to the list. But I prefer to focus my energy on a more positive approach—tackle these challenges and demonstrate how sharing can benefit the work you do. The bottom line is that educators must work together to create a culture of sharing.

HOW EDUCATORS CAN SOLVE THE CHALLENGES OF SHARING

COLLABORATION: THE ORGANIC MENTORSHIP

One of the criticisms I have heard most often from teachers with just a few years in the classroom is they felt like they were "fed to the wolves." If new teachers simply receive a list of topics to cover, a textbook, or even a curriculum map, educators aren't doing enough to encourage collaboration. Educators need to do a better job of creating a culture of sharing so a new teacher immediately notices collaboration as a tangible part of what the teachers do. I did not understand the power of collaboration among colleagues until a few years into my teaching career, and I only found it by accident. For me, a new friendship with a new colleague is what gave me an opportunity to experience collaboration with another teacher. It happened naturally because we were friends. Interestingly enough, another teacher in the building became incredibly frustrated with the team that year. This person felt as though the school really believed in teacher collaboration and sharing, but that it wasn't happening in our department. Hearing her say that was the first time anyone brought to my attention that sharing was the norm, because as a person new to the building, I hadn't previously felt that to be the case. Perception is reality, so we have to be intentional about the culture we are introducing to new-to-teaching or new-to-the-building teachers.

Does your school have a formal or informal mentorship program? If not, how else can a culture of sharing become a part of how you support and mentor teachers who are new to your building? This is especially important because many new teachers likely experience what many seasoned educators have: survival mode. Survival mode is real. I would have drowned if others hadn't been willing to share and help me. Understandably, some new teachers may not be in a place where they are ready or able to share; however, they might be in the perfect spot to accept sharing. Everything will come full circle when they are ready to share with someone else.

PERCEPTION IS REALITY, SO WE HAVE TO BE INTENTIONAL ABOUT THE CULTURE WE ARE INTRODUCING TO NEW-TO-TEACHING OR NEW-TO-THE-BUILDING TEACHERS.

· · · · · · · · · · ·

When I was a new teacher at a new building, I was part of a discussion with my department in which another teacher criticized us as a group because we weren't in the habit of sharing materials with each other. The teacher mentioned that she had seen a cool activity in the printer entitled "Mimicking Melinda," a characterization activity tied in with *Speak*, a book several of us taught. I was excited and flattered because I had created the activity. I shared with the group that I had created the item and I was happy to share it. But it was a "one and done" sharing situation; I missed the point entirely. It hadn't occurred to me to share what I had created with the established teachers, for several reasons—one of them being I was insecure, fearful that doing so would communicate that I believed what I had to offer was better than what they were using.

Another teacher in the department admitted she hadn't been sharing items because we didn't have a culture of sharing. I felt I had been given items at the beginning of the year, but no one was reaching out regularly. I hadn't discovered a PLN yet and didn't realize what I was missing by working mostly on my own. While at another building that I worked in as a classroom teacher, I felt that the other teachers in my department were readily sharing with me and each other. I wouldn't have survived without that culture. So, what creates a culture of sharing? What is it about some cultures that leave us working and creating in isolation?

A SHARED PROCESS FOR VETTING HIGH-QUALITY CONTENT

As you become better at finding high-quality content, you become more skilled at creating high-quality content, and vice versa. Writers will say if you want to become a great writer, you should read great writers. And you better believe it when a great writer recommends one of their favorites. (I only read Harlan Coben because Stephen King recommended him!) If you can work together with your department, school, and district to agree on what you want to see in your content, you can look for nonnegotiables such as accessibility, levels of student interaction, depth of knowledge (DOK), etc. When you do this, you know that the content you are sharing meets your expectations.

TIME TO SHARE-JAM SESSIONS

Another request I have heard from so many educators is simply to be given time to share with others in their content area. Think about what would happen if teachers were given this time and came to the table with a great activity or lesson they had created and were ready to share. Likely those conversations would spark new—and even better—ideas! Everyone would leave with a handful of new ideas to take back to their classrooms, new connections to draw on in the future, and new ideas to create in the future—none of which would have happened without the time to sit together and share.

PEER REVIEW

Another way to tackle challenges related to sharing is through a peer review process. For example, many schools in Indiana use the virtual option for inclement weather through the Department of Education. This gives schools flexibility in making up missed school days—a norm for us because of the frequency of snow, freezing rain, and even fog. When schools begin to take advantage of this virtual option, many of them ask teachers to create online lessons and submit them to administrators for feedback before they go live with the content. If peer review also were part of this process, teachers would have a built-in arena for sharing. And then, what if peer review became part of how you designed content every day? Your administrators likely encourage you to observe other educators as part of your continued learning, and a process for peer review of instructional materials is another way to "observe" other educators. By doing this, you have another way to view what is working for others in the classroom. Not only will you be able to provide meaningful feedback to your peer review partner, your partner will have a natural way to share tools, tricks, and ideas with you that you can then apply to the items you create.

COLLABORATIVE CREATION

Get into the habit of creating with others. Administrators, create your professional learning with another administrator or—even better—with a teacher. Teachers, create your instructional materials with another teacher, or even include students in the process. In my experience, though perhaps yours has been different, I see more collaboration happening in elementary grade-level teams than I experienced as a secondary teacher. A PLN that creates together learns together.

ASKING FOR CREDIT!

Earlier, I mentioned a friend who was totally okay with me using his work without giving him credit at all. I also shared that in some situations, I've openly given permission for others to use my work—no credit necessary. But, I also understand wanting to get credit for your hard work, too. And while I try to keep myself grounded in my role by remembering the Truman quote, "It is amazing what you can accomplish if you do not care who gets the credit," it is okay to want to get credit, too. Share, but ask that others acknowledge you when using your resource. If you are the creator, you should feel comfortable about what happens to your resource when it leaves your hands. And while we have to admit this isn't a foolproof process and we can't control what others ultimately do, we can and should feel okay asking for credit by including Creative Commons (CC) licenses with our work. Creative Commons licenses can help us have conversations about how we'd like to see our stuff used. (More about this is coming!) Get into the habit of giving credit for what you use, and be loud about it so others see it and take notice!

PART FOUR:
RECOGNIZE

=

Give Credit

CHAPTER 12
Copyright 101

In general, the word "copyright" may have negative connotations. It has gotten a bad rap for its "I gotcha" quality. But I would like for us to give copyright a break and let it shine for what it really is: a way to encourage creators to create. As a classroom teacher, you have options about how you can apply copyright to your classroom. You might choose to apply fair use guidelines or you might turn to the Face to Face Teaching exemption. If you do any sort of distance instruction or virtual instruction, you might look to the TEACH Act. Different guidelines apply to different classroom scenarios. It is important for you to understand the larger scope of this and what is specifically applicable to you as a classroom teacher.

An interesting conversation surrounding the copyrighting of dance moves and the video game phenomenon Fortnite has pushed this topic of copyright to the surface. If you perform a Google phrase search for "Fortnite copyright," you will locate a number of articles published on the topic. This discussion raises a list of questions:

- Who owns performed choreography?
- How can you prove you created a dance move?
- Can you copyright dance moves?
- Can you trademark a dance move?

People want credit for the content and works they create, and although some take this more seriously than others, creators do deserve to decide what happens to their work. This is just one example of many illustrating how quickly you can get into the weeds when discussing this topic.

Although the US Copyright Law clearly outlines that choreography is eligible for copyright protection, Fortnite is making the argument that they are simply using single dance moves—not choreographed strings of several dance moves qualifying for copyright protection. I have had moments when I wonder, "Wait, have I heard this before?" or "Where did I learn this?" You can become hypersensitive to copyright once it is on your radar.

Copyright contains two messages. The first is about how you can honor copyright law and intellectual property, and the second is what you can do when someone violates your property. In education, the first part matters most. My hope is that you are more concerned with creating and sharing than you are with catching mistakes. And if mistakes do happen in a public school setting, I also don't think it is appropriate to go after educators, schools, or districts with an iron fist.

WHAT IS COPYRIGHT?

Copyright by definition is a "form of protection grounded in the US Constitution and granted by law for original works of authorship fixed in a tangible medium of expression. Copyright covers both published and unpublished works."[1]

Throughout the years, copyright law has evolved and continues to evolve in response to our changing culture and access to technology. For example, the length of copyright protection for a work has changed several times. The first copyright law went into effect in 1790.[2] Originally, creators had the right to protect their work for a period of fourteen years. Currently, copyrighted works are protected for the life of the author plus seventy years, as a result of the Sonny Bono Copyright Term Extension Act.[3] Our current version of copyright law was enacted in 1976 and "extended federal copyright protection to all works, both published and unpublished, once they are fixed in a tangible form."[4]

A work is copyright protected once it exists. You might imagine that a creator has to apply for a copyright or register a work for copyright to apply, but this is not the case. When a creator creates something new and tangible, whatever the medium, copyright is implied without any additional steps. Creators do not need to register or apply to receive copyright protection of a creation, although there is a process for registering a work if the creator chooses to do so.

Copyright protection extends to numerous media—beyond the scope many may assume; for example, works of authorship include the following categories:

(1) literary works

(2) musical works, including any accompanying words

(3) dramatic works, including any accompanying music

(4) pantomimes and choreographic works

(5) pictorial, graphic, and sculptural works

(6) motion pictures and other audiovisual works

(7) sound recordings

(8) architectural works[5]

This portion of the copyright code also specifies that copyright protects creative works—not ideas—regardless of how the ideas are expressed.

Copyright, patents, and trademarks are not synonymous with one another. Copyright protects original, creative works. Patents protect inventions. Trademarks protect items that lead us back to the source of a product, such as a slogan or a logo.

Just as information literacy skills ask, you have to be sure the sources telling you an item is okay to use are reliable. YouTube is a perfect example. Even if someone else has made the decision to share something, you need to be sure that you should be using it. The Internet is full of examples of items that should never have been shared in the first place. If you use something in your classroom that you should not, regardless of whether you are aware of the error, you are continuing a culture that does not respect intellectual and creative property. Is copyright something you can apply the "ask for forgiveness, not permission" approach to? Probably not, although I think most educators would admit they've been there. You should always assume everything is copyright protected unless you have specific information that shows how something is licensed. Only the copyright holder can grant us permission if we would like to use something outside of the scope that copyright exemptions allow us.

WHOSE RESPONSIBILITY IS IT?

If you are an educator, you are likely very skilled at prioritizing your work. So many things fly at you from all directions simultaneously. With all of the things you must sift through, if you aren't intentional about what you choose to focus on, something you categorize as "extra" will be pushed to the back burner. When it comes to copyright, however, it would be unwise to allow this to happen—especially if you are in a leadership role. Copyright cannot be treated as an "extra." Convincing evidence is available to show why and how districts should be supporting teachers in their understanding and application of copyright as it relates to designing digital content.

IF YOU USE SOMETHING IN YOUR CLASSROOM THAT YOU SHOULD NOT, REGARDLESS OF WHETHER YOU ARE AWARE OF THE ERROR, YOU ARE CONTINUING A CULTURE THAT DOES NOT RESPECT INTELLECTUAL AND CREATIVE PROPERTY.

Title II of the Digital Millennium Copyright Act of 1998 addresses the Online Copyright Infringement Liability Limitation. This is the limitation protecting online platforms such as YouTube from being responsible for the infringements their contributors make when they upload content to the site. Particularly interesting is that this limitation can give schools guidance and can help answer the question of who is responsible for copyright violations within a school setting.

This limitation includes special rules regarding the liability of nonprofit educational institutions. Specifically,

> [Section 512(e)] determines when the actions or knowledge of a faculty member or graduate student employee who is performing a teaching or research function may affect the eligibility of a nonprofit educational institution for one of the four limitations on liability. As to the limitations for transitory communications or system caching, the faculty member or student shall be considered a "person other than the provider," so as to avoid disqualifying the institution from eligibility. As to the other limitations, the knowledge or awareness of the faculty member or student will not be attributed to the institution. The following conditions must be met:
>
> • The faculty member or graduate student's infringing activities do not involve providing online access to course

materials that were required or recommended during the past three years.

- The institution has not received more than two notifications over the past three years that the faculty member or graduate student was infringing.

- The institution provides all of its users with informational materials describing and promoting compliance with copyright law.[6]

The conclusion educators can draw from this is that schools and districts have a responsibility to educate and support teachers in this realm, especially if districts do not want to be held responsible for any copyright violations. Although I don't believe in a fear-based approach on this, likely educators would be lying if they said the value of "covering their butts" wasn't on their minds with this. No one wants to be called out for copyright violations. No one wants to get themselves or their school or district into any type of trouble. Districts and schools must offer education and guidance on copyright. It is simply foundational to what we are asked to do as educators every day. If districts meet these conditions, they are protecting themselves while building the skillset for teachers so they are also protected. The intention should be less about districts covering their derrieres and more about supporting teachers when asking them to design digital content. This is a win-win.

Perform a phrase search in Google using the phrase "copyright lawsuit school" or any similar search, and you will quickly uncover a plethora of copyright lawsuits involving teachers, districts, and schools. The cases range from the unpermitted use of images on school websites, to the stealing and reproduction of licensed textbook materials, to the irresponsible broadcasting of a film. I don't want to give this too much space, but educators know these are real issues happening in their schools. You have to protect yourself, your school, and your students. You have to protect your students from making these mistakes in an online world as a proactive approach to their future. Educators must respond to the changes they have seen in education within the past twenty years that are making them more vulnerable than ever before. You have to see your role as ever changing and adapt your skillset to meet the requirements of a successful educator today. A thorough understanding of copyright is one of these skills.

ARE TEACHERS THE BIGGEST PLAGIARIZERS?

I've also heard people claim that teachers are the biggest plagiarizers. While this most likely comes from our over-application of fair use, it is a very real issue. When people call teachers out for being the "biggest plagiarizers," administrators need to consider what they have done to put their teachers in this survival-mode situation. And survival mode is the reason. No teacher sits down to plan a lesson and thinks, "Hmm, how can I intentionally plagiarize and break copyright laws today?" Real-life education equates to teachers with large classes. Teachers have to plan for three, four, five—or even more—different courses each day. Teachers have been told to supplement using digital materials or, in some cases, have had textbooks stripped away to save money, with little to no direction on how to find supplemental materials for their classes. The bottom line is that teachers are doing the best they can with the time, support, and materials they have. Unfortunately, at times, this isn't enough and does lead to educators breaking some of the rules to get the job done. You've likely experienced this personally.

In other cases, though, teachers' plagiarism isn't about survival mode. Inspired educators come to work ready to be creative, engage students, and break the mold of traditional education but make similar mistakes. They use images and memes to make presentations more appealing—without citing a single one. Teachers use YouTube videos (and in some cases download them to show later if their school web filtering doesn't make YouTube available) in any number of instructional strategies. My guess is that you can think of a time you did something for the sake of your students, knowing it was probably not quite in line with fair use and copyright laws. I have asked countless educators how closely they consider copyright and fair use when planning lessons. Some educators share that they simply do not feel confident knowing how to address this topic. Others state that they won't get in trouble, so they don't worry about it (although there is plenty of evidence to the contrary). Some are bold and claim they knowingly break those rules but frankly do not care because they will do what is best for students. While this a spirit I can get behind, I still want to unpack this response a bit! The truth is, you can do both.

Educators need to shift their perspective a bit. Yes, I'm saying you can accomplish creating engaging activities and follow fair use and copyright. The two are not mutually exclusive. In fact, I'll go so far as to say you will find yourself creating even richer experiences because you're doing so through the lens of copyright.

COPY AND PASTE

I let my advanced composition students copy and paste. Please hear me out before judging too harshly.

When I first started teaching, research was an event. We had to leave the classroom and travel to a computer lab or media center. We took notes on paper or notecards (gasp!). As access to more technology grew and teachers took advantage of opportunities for students to research and write on a device, writing instructors everywhere started to debate: Do we ditch the notecards and bibliography cards? I have taught the process of writing using many methods, and I have tried different mediums, including both paper 3×5 notecards and digital notecards. As I continued to examine my position on this debate, I asked myself to focus on the skills I was attempting to build in my students. I wanted them to be masters of letting the research guide the claims they made. I wanted them to be skilled in analyzing research and using it to support the points the paper held. Typing direct quotes verbatim wasn't something I was concerned about—so I told them to copy and paste.

YOU WILL FIND YOURSELF CREATING EVEN RICHER EXPERIENCES BECAUSE YOU'RE DOING SO THROUGH THE LENS OF COPYRIGHT.

Educators use the phrase copy and paste regularly as if it were synonymous with plagiarism. But the act of copying and pasting itself isn't bad. Instead, plagiarism occurs when writers attempt to pass off another's work or ideas as their own. Copying and pasting a paragraph, or even a line, without proper citation is plagiarism. By contrast, copying and pasting a direct quote from a source, adding citations, and including it as part of a larger work is just good time management. Copying and pasting isn't bad; a lack of citations is. Your intentions are what must be called into question.

If you are an English teacher (and probably other content area teachers can relate), you have most likely heard the old "but I changed some of the words" excuse when confronting a student accused of plagiarism. A misconception exists when we tell students they can steal something— whether they copy and paste it or not—and plead the Fifth as long as they change some words around or throw in a synonym or two. This is not true.

Plagiarism is the theft of ideas. Copyright protects the products of our ideas come to life. Citation and attribution are the first defenses toward protecting intellectual property. This is nothing new. Teachers have been holding their students accountable for citing evidence since . . . always.

But who is responsible for requiring the citation of evidence that students use in coursework? Answer: Every single educator. Students know whether a teacher expects citations and the application of information literacy skills. Respecting and protecting intellectual and creative property is always essential. But why do we require citations when students are doing larger projects or research papers and diminish its importance within smaller tasks?

ALL TEACHERS SHOULD ALL HOLD THEIR STUDENTS— AND EACH OTHER—TO THE EXPECTATION OF APPLYING COPYRIGHT

The use of computers in the classroom used to be an event; it was separate from what was happening in the classroom. But this has changed as the use of technology as a tool to learn has become somewhat constant. Applying copyright and being a good digital citizen shouldn't be seen as an event or as something important only when you are deciding to focus on it as a "one and done." It needs to become a constant in your classrooms. You might shift the format, depending on the content area, but the expectation to cite should be there regardless. Educators can work together across content areas to determine what their norms should look like. The English teachers might be responsible for providing some skill building in this realm, but all teachers should all hold their students—and each other— to the expectation of applying copyright and the protection of intellectual property in literally everything they create using existing material.

To aid students in this process, I've attempted many methods. I've used a Google Doc as a table to collect quotes and citation information. I've created notecard templates using Google Slides for my students to use as a substitute for paper ones. I've allowed them to print resources so they could highlight and annotate. My conclusion, ultimately, is that educators must help their students advocate for a process they can embrace and relate to as they become mature writers.

CHAPTER 13
An Introduction to Attribution: Images

Schools are using digital content today more than ever before. As a result of 1:1 teaching environments, schools are relying on digital resources, open educational resources, and teacher-created content to support curricular goals. As more content is pushed out to students through online platforms, educators' responsibility to consider copyright as part of their planning process—no matter what the process looks like—grows.

When educators consider adding the responsibility of copyright, their first hurdle is time. When they are in the trenches of testing windows, grading, school safety—and their other responsibilities—copyright may not feel like their first priority. But it must become a priority. Educators must invest time and effort into becoming comfortable applying copyright, not only to keep themselves free of the consequences of not doing so, but also to pass on these skills to their students. Often when I begin to discuss copyright with educators, many respond with a bit of fear in their eyes, asking, "Does this mean I have to redo everything I've ever done?" Not at all!

"I DID THEN WHAT I KNEW HOW TO DO. NOW THAT I KNOW BETTER, I DO BETTER"
—MAYA ANGELOU

Do you feel intimidated? Scared? Don't be! Copyright contains many moving pieces to think about, and much of it lives in the gray area. Instead of trying to tackle it all at once, commit yourself to making one change at a time. Images are the perfect place to start.

No matter their role, educators use images in the content they create. They include images on instructional materials, students are encouraged to use images as part of their work, and administrators frequently publish information for a community audience, often complete with images. The practice of doing a quick Google image search to locate these images or one to use for a school mascot logo on the school website has to change. Knowing this will also help you be more intentional about how you are using images in the work you create and how you are asking students to use images in the work they create. If you are using an image in instructional materials, shouldn't it have an instructional purpose? When we use images simply for the sake of making something look nice, we may be causing the resource to be less functional; high-quality design can be another fringe benefit to designing with copyright in mind.

NO MATTER THEIR ROLE, EDUCATORS USE IMAGES IN THE CONTENT THEY CREATE.

Respecting intellectual property is something students should learn to practice and value before leaving our classrooms, but educators cannot support their students in learning these skills until they learn and implement them personally. So, where should educators start?

CREATIVE COMMONS LICENSING

Enter Creative Commons. Creative Commons sparks and embodies much of what I share in this book. Creative Commons encourages the sharing of creative content and intellectual property in a way to both honor the creator and support remixes of originals into something new.

Creative Commons also makes copyright easy to navigate. A large majority of educators likely don't consider themselves to be confident in all areas of copyright. Creative Commons allows educators to work smarter by using a system to support them in the areas they don't want or need to be experts on. Simply using the Creative Commons system, either to license your own work or to attribute work you find licensed under Creative Commons, helps you build your understanding of copyright.

Creative Commons provides a couple of services: First, it helps creators navigate and manage the elements of copyright as it applies to their own creative works. For example, if teachers create a lesson and want to share, but want to be more specific about how the lesson is used in other class-rooms, they can use a Creative Commons license and apply it to their work. Second, Creative Commons maintains a platform for searching items, using the Creative Commons licenses (https://search.creativecommons.org). Additionally, you will see Creative Commons licenses on items throughout several platforms, and most of these are platforms you will recognize such as YouTube and Flickr.

As a creator, Creative Commons licensing helps you control how your work is used and shared. Although my hope is that you feel inspired to share the instructional content you create with others, you don't want to be taken advantage of either. Striking the balance between these two is something educators won't always come to a consensus on.

Think of it like filtering the Internet. An Information Technology (IT) department will never be able to make filtering decisions to make one hun-dred percent of a teaching and administrative staff happy. Some educators prefer to keep the Internet locked down tight, hoping it will make classroom management easier, and others want it to be completely open to students, focusing on building digital citizenship skills. (I tend to believe in filtering as the law requires and letting the engagement in my classroom do the rest.) So instead of constantly trying to worry about how to filter the Internet in a way to serve everyone and keep them happy, an IT department finds a tool to give everyone a certain level of autonomy instead. Quite a few Internet filtering tools that schools adopt use a default policy agreed on by leader-ship, and teachers can then tighten or loosen the filtering policy depending on the day, assignment, or classroom dynamics. This is a great system.

Think of this as parallel to educators sharing materials. We don't have to agree on how our content should be used and shared, and individuals should also feel okay about changing their minds depending on the sce-nario. My friend Mark truly did not mind if his stuff was shared and used— even without credit. He cared more about his colleagues doing well, and this prompted him to continue to share, knowing his materials were being used by other educators and, ultimately, reaching more students than they would have otherwise. Other educators are willing to share but prefer those using the materials to give credit back to them. Creators also might feel strongly that the items they share not be used by another for profit. If they are selflessly sharing, others should not be able to make money off of work they did not originally bring to life. You might find yourself falling distinctly into one of these categories, but no group is more right than another. The preference is impacted by a number of variables, and a creator should have the ability to decide how items are used, as long as they are willing to share with and support one another. Personally, I consider a number of factors when deciding how to share my work, and I use a couple of different licenses. Creative Commons is the tool educators can use to "default" to a system that is fair to everyone while giving creators some space for autonomy. Creative Commons is a way to filter, if you will, what the life of educators' works look like after they leave their hands.

A unique and incredibly cool feature of the Creative Commons licenses is that they are customizable—almost like the a la carte section of a cafeteria. You can choose the items you like and piece them together to make you feel confident about the way you license your work. It is the ripple effect in motion—the simple flap of a butterfly's wing to continue to shift the culture of how teachers create, share, and see themselves.

Applying copyright through images you use does require you to make a shift—a shift in where you go to search for images, your process for choosing images, and how you ultimately give credit for images you use. Following these four steps can help you navigate the process:

Shift where you look. Use Creative Commons to search for images. Get into the habit of using the Commons to locate the images you use. Using this platform allows you to filter specifically for items you can use commercially or items labeled to modify. This search will give you results across several websites. You can also focus your search by filtering to only get results from specific sites; for example, you might choose to look for images only within Flickr. For additional ideas of where to look for openly licensed images, head to dianargill.com!

Locate licensing information. Make locating the licensing information for each image part of your process. Using the Commons to search for images will help you in your process of properly attributing. However, simply using the Commons to search does not necessarily guarantee that what you find is free to use. Make it a habit to check how each image you use is licensed. The location of the license depends on the platform, but generally speaking, you should be able to find it below the image.

Get to know the Creative Commons licenses. Creative Commons licenses allow the licensor to be specific about how others use materials.

Once you locate the license information for an image, the next step is to determine which of the Creative Commons licenses has been applied. The license will give you specific guidance on how the image can be used. A license may include elements to prohibit modification (noderivatives), forbid reuse for commercial purposes (noncommercial), or require that you also share the new work you have included the image within (share alike). The only license not requiring attribution is "CC0," meaning licensors waive their rights to the work. This is similar to the way you might cite an item from the public domain.

Include image attributions in all of your materials. "Best Practice for Attribution"[1] (wiki.creativecommons.org/wiki/Best_practices_for_attribution) direct users to include four items: title, author, source, and license. Users should also hyperlink back to the source of the image, the author's page, and include a link to the Creative Commons license as part of the attribution.

Below is an example of a properly attributed image licensed for reuse. As a side note, I search using the term "giraffe" one hundred percent of the time when demonstrating search techniques for educators and students alike. Performing a live Google search can be scary, but "giraffe" has never done me wrong.

"Chester Zoo" by Nigel Swales - 2 is licensed under CC BY-SA 2.0

The image of the giraffe and boy is an example of one licensed under a Simplified Pixabay License, and no attribution is required. In an effort to model, though, I typically attribute when I have the information or make a note of the license anyway. (Really, I just love this picture and wanted to include it. Really, really...I just love giraffes.)

Using these four steps can help you start applying copyright in an immediately relevant way for your students and yourself. The next time you create a new resource, find your visual media using Creative Commons and provide proper attributions. The next time you ask students to create an infographic or a ThingLink, direct them to do the same. If this is the only change you make for a while, it is a huge step toward shifting your process!

Will educators continue to use images they should not be using in their materials without much thought of retribution? Of course. However, now you have a few simple steps to incorporate into your creative process to improve your copyright skills, model best practices for each other and your students, and ultimately, help your students consider copyright as part of their own creative process. Again—know better, do better.

One of my favorite activities to do with students or educators as an introduction to the Creative Commons licenses has two parts. First, we find something licensed using CC licenses and practice proper attribution. Second, we create something and attach a license to it.

The first activity (I call it "find and use") takes participants through the process of locating an image licensed using the Creative Commons licenses, creating something with the image, and providing proper attribution. This practical exercise introduces them to licensing lingo and lets them apply the process in the same way they might in real life. For a student, this could be creating something for class. For a teacher, it could be creating a digital activity or instructional materials.

To get started, I share a collaborative space with the group, usually an editable Google Slides presentation. Then I give a prompt. For example,

Imagine you are a new member of The Beastie Boys, and you need to create a slide that shares your hip hop moniker and that introduces yourself as a new Beastie. Be sure to include an image that represents who you are as a Beastie, and provide proper attribution.

With teacher groups, I especially enjoy giving them the prompt to create a meme about their classroom. To do so, they have to find an image licensed for reuse and modification. In the process, we get to have a conversation about how we can leverage the power of memes without violating copyright! It's a simple exercise, but we love to create. See? Copyright education doesn't have to be stuffy and serious. Instead, it can be a door to creativity! I encourage you to try an exercise like this with your staff or your students.

The second activity asks students or staff to create something entirely new. Using Google Slides or Google Drawings, students can create a product or graphic entirely from scratch and decide how they want their new item to be shared and used in the future. Consider finding time for teachers to get together, and ask everyone to bring their most favorite lesson they created or remixed. Before facilitating a group share, introduce the Creative Commons licenses, ask teachers to decide how they want their work licensed, encourage everyone to add a license, and then everyone can share. What a powerful way to honor teachers as instructional designers and professionals!

OTHER PLACES TO FIND IMAGES
FINDING IMAGES WITH GSUITE TOOLS

GSuite tools have always been my favorite for many reasons, including versatility and safety for all ages. The power of collaborative creativity they provide, however, is what really makes them stand out among the rest.

When you create in GSuite tools, you will discover that Google has thoughtfully and responsibly made the process of choosing images to use in your creations incredibly user friendly. Without a doubt, this is my favorite way to instruct students. I also prefer to have students use this process over doing an advanced Google image search, because it keeps them working within their creative space.

A stand-alone mini lesson on copyright and images might have its place, but helping students understand copyright in a way that is immediately applicable is even more powerful. The same goes for adult learning, too!

While working within Google Slides, Google Drawings, Google Docs, and Google Forms, etc., select insert > image > search the web.

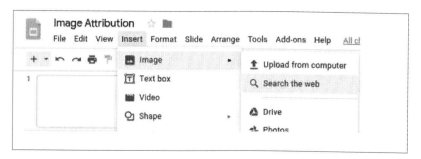

A Google image search dashboard will pop up on the right side of your screen. From there, you can perform a keyword search or a phrase search to look for your visual media.

After performing your search, you will see a tiny magnifying glass icon in the bottom right corner of each image thumbnail. Click this to preview an image.

The preview of the image will show you two things. At the very top, you will find a link back to the image source. You can use this to get all of the information you need for proper attribution and to double-check the licensing information. Under the image, you will see the license information, but Google does remind you it is on you to be certain that you are using the image as the licensing allows.

If I have decided I want to use the image, the next step in the process is to click on the source link above it, insert the image, and provide attribution before moving on. I find it is much easier to take care of attribution right away instead of trying to find the source later on.

Head to my website for resources you can use to guide students through these steps!

GOOGLE ADVANCED SEARCH

If you are using Google Images to search for media content or are directing students to do so, a couple of steps will ensure that your search results include only items you can responsibly and safely use in your creative content.

After navigating to trusty Google, choose Images, perform a search, and look at the top of the page. You will see an option for settings>advanced search. (By the way, in true Google fashion, there are other ways to get here, so choose your path and make it happen.)

Scroll down until you get to Usage Rights. From there, you can select the filter to best fit your situation for what you are using and creating. I typically select "free to use share or modify," because it's likely I will crop the image into a cute little shape, but I don't plan to sell anything. Teachers give teachers, am I right?!

Disclaimer here: this will seriously impact your ability to locate memes. Your students will notice this. They will notice the difference between a free and unfiltered Google Image Search and one filtered for usage rights. This is one of the reasons I prefer to direct students to do essentially the same thing, but within the GSuite tools themselves. I have done mini lessons on this many times. The students are watching me, and they are hearing me. They try it, and then they go right back to an unfiltered search to find their images, because they want what they want! And if they want memes, what a fabulous opportunity to encourage them to create their own—using openly licensed images, of course!

Head to my site for templates and Slides presentations to help you teach this skill!

SEARCHING FOR IMAGES USING CREATIVE COMMONS

The Creative Commons "search 'the commons'" option is an excellent place to find images because it acts as a list of platforms working with the Creative Commons licenses. This also provides another great lesson in information literacy, because it requires you to consider which search engine would be most appropriate for the search you are performing to locate the content you want.

Encourage students to use the Creative Commons platforms when finding content to use for class creations. Students will recognize the platforms working with Creative Commons (Flickr, YouTube). Mastering the art of properly attributing content leads to students licensing their own content in the future.

After navigating to creativecommons.org, click **Search for CC images**. From there you can decide what type of license you need to create what you have in mind by selecting the appropriate checkboxes. The old search portal also allows you to choose which platform you want to search.

Pixabay is a favorite of mine, because the images are licensed so that no attribution at all is required! Personally, I still go through the steps of providing an attribution to model, but I think this is a great sell for students and adults. People love things to make their lives easier, so why wouldn't they love Pixabay? And it still opens the door to having conversations about responsible use and the protection of creative property. If students thoughtfully go to Pixabay to find images, instead of doing an unfiltered Google search, because they know it will be easier to search only for images not requiring attribution, they certainly have the topic of copyright in mind!

Creative Commons also has an incredible tool to allow for one-click attribution. This is a cool new feature to aid in the process of attribution by making it entirely painless. (This is a very Carrie Bradshaw "Hello, lover!" moment for me—but without the shoes!) This feature is currently (spring 2019) in beta and only includes the one-click attribution for image content. This allows you to perform a keyword search to locate an image. Once you select an image and click on it, the Creative Commons licensing information is clearly outlined under the image. Remember, no matter what, it is on you to be sure that the image is okay to use, and you can verify that it is by following the links provided back to the source. You can copy and paste a completed, perfectly formatted, and hyperlinked attribution for the image. Even better, you can simply click "copy rich text," and you can paste the beautiful attribution wherever it needs to go. So—much—YES!

The Noun Project is another great place to find graphics to include as part of your digital content, and the licensing of the images to simplify their use. The Noun Project curates literally millions of icons licensed with Creative Commons licenses. You can use these icons "as is" with attribution or you can purchase a yearly subscription allowing you to use the icons as royalty-free, modifiable images. You also can purchase individual licenses for one graphic at a time.

MAKE YOUR OWN IMAGES

As you start to view yourself as a designer and creator, why not let this carry over into the images you use within your digital content, too? So many digital tools make it simple to design from scratch, and when you create your own images, you can consider copyright from the creator's perspective. Tools such as Canva.com can make it seem like you are a well-trained graphic designer. The templates help you get started, or you can start with a clean canvas and use the tools within it to create something fabulous. I love to use this tool to give my materials my own branded look. (Be sure to read the Canva.com terms of use to know exactly how you can use the tool and images!) Another great tool for creating your own images is Google

Drawings. Inserting shapes and overlapping them to create something new is a good way to get started. There are tons of YouTube tutorials to help you get creative with Google Drawings to design your own images. One of my favorites helps you turn a photograph into a color-blocked pop-art masterpiece! Google Slides is another tool I love to use for design. By simply changing the dimensions of the slide so it is a square and dropping in some text and shapes, I can create an original image for a social media campaign, a logo, or whatever I need to give my materials their signature look. Think about the possibilities of this for your students. If you can't find an openly licensed image to meet your needs, then you have stumbled onto the perfect opportunity to create.

IF YOU CAN'T FIND AN OPENLY LICENSED IMAGE TO MEET YOUR NEEDS, THEN YOU HAVE STUMBLED ONTO THE PERFECT OPPORTUNITY TO CREATE.

. . . .

Check out the site for some fun design templates in Slides and a PD session on Canva that you can use!

CHAPTER 14
Film, Video, and Copyright

Most would agree that a magical connection exists between art and memories. When you hear a song, does it remind you of the specific time in your life when it was popular? Or did a meaningful song help you get through a tough time? The same can be said about films, too. I remember the movie I saw with my friends the day after senior prom, the first dinner and movie date my husband took me on, and the first film I took each of my children to (even though I don't remember the story of the movie because my kids had to pee five hundred times!).

Both movies and music have a place in the classroom, providing a similar "magical" connection experience. They can help educators connect with their students and help make the connection more human. They can also enrich the classroom experiences that educators design for their students.

CAN I SHOW THIS MOVIE?

If images were the best place to start when considering copyright in the classroom, film should be next on your list. Let me throw a few scenarios at you:

- It's the end of the quarter, and winter break starts tomorrow. You are thinking of rewarding your students with the gift of watching a movie in class (while you get a bit of grading done at the same time!).

- Your students just finished a novel, and you want them to watch the movie. Of course, you will compare and contrast the film and the novel.

- An after-school club wants to have a movie night, but they won't be charging admission.

Not all of the scenarios can be called examples of fair use, in line with the face-to-face teaching exemption, or in accordance with copyright law, and certainly not all of them are examples of high-quality instruction, either. Am I guilty of at least one of these examples? Yes. Did I miss an opportunity for some engaging learning? Probably. For me, this last point is the most important. If you ask, "Can I show this movie in class?" I think you are asking the wrong question. It would be better to shift the question to, "What resources would best help my students achieve mastery of the skills I am supporting them in?"

If a film or part of a film answers this question, you are remembering to stay true to your actual goals, and your shift in internal dialogue allows you to make sound instructional decisions. Because this conversation can be difficult, instead of getting too deep in the mud about what you shouldn't do with film, consider some ideas to leverage your knowledge of the face-to-face teaching exemption (described below). I also want to remind you to allow yourself some grace with this one. Your intentions are good. You want your students to have memorable experiences! In fact, one of the most influential teachers I had as a student loved his legacy of showing a powerful movie each year before Christmas Break. Will watching a film for fun harm your students? Probably not. Can we do better? Of course! And when it comes to copyright in the classroom, once you know better, you have to do better!

As with any decision you make for your students, the one of how to use film or video in your classes should be done intentionally. Ask yourself several questions as you evaluate the decision:

- How and why are you choosing to use film?
- What learning goals are you aiming to accomplish through viewing films?
- How will your students learn from and interact with the video content?
- How can your students use the viewing of film to create something new?

AS WITH ANY DECISION YOU MAKE FOR YOUR STUDENTS, THE ONE OF HOW TO USE FILM OR VIDEO IN YOUR CLASSES SHOULD BE DONE INTENTIONALLY.

. . . .

Aim to use the smallest amount of copyrighted material to achieve your instructional goals. The materials you select should be used as part of direct instruction. When you consider how to successfully use film in your classroom, particularly in blended learning environments, best practices suggest that simply asking students to view a film—whether a clip from a movie, an instructional video from YouTube, or something you create using your document camera—isn't successful. Learning becomes powerful when students interact with content. The process of considering fair use and copyright isn't only about protecting yourself. It can become a regular part of your planning process and can assist you in designing experiences intentionally.

All educators still ask, "Can I show my kids this movie?" Section 110 of Section 17 of US Copyright Law, referred to as the "Face-to-Face Teaching Exemption," shares a specific exemption giving you direction for how film can be used in the classroom:

> ...the following are not infringements of copyright: (1) performance or display of a work by instructors or pupils in the course of face-to-face teaching activities of a nonprofit educational institution, in a classroom or similar place devoted to instruction, unless, in the case of a motion picture or other audiovisual work, the performance, or the display of individual images, is given by means of a copy that was not lawfully made under this title, and that the person responsible for the performance knew or had reason to believe was not lawfully made.[1]

To summarize, this exception allows educators to show films in their classrooms as part of face-to-face teaching. This exemption does not apply to movies shown online as part of a brick-and-mortar course or as part of a virtual course; these practices would put you in violation. The content of the film should be directly related to or essential to the core curriculum of the course. A teacher should be able to make a strong case in defense of using a film in class as part of direct instruction. In addition, the exemption says if you knowingly show a film copied unlawfully, for example, the exemption no longer applies, and you are knowingly breaking copyright laws. (Don't get me started on those Amazon Firestick tricks!)

Schools are often the center of their communities, and they organize events and fundraisers—like movie night—going outside the scope of the curriculum. When a school considers showing a film as part of one of these events, the same rules apply. Even if you rent, borrow from a library, or even purchase a film, you would be in violation of copyright if you show it as a public performance—even if the location is a school.

Through the questions and conversations I have surrounding this topic, I find the biggest misconception is that as long as schools aren't charging people a fee to attend and watch the film, they are not in violation of copyright. Even nonprofit organizations need a public performance license, regardless of the presence or absence of an admission cost. An event such as this isn't tied to direct instruction, and you aren't using the film in a classroom setting, meaning fair use or the face-to-face teaching exemption most likely won't apply to any of these situations. In these instances, schools need to consider purchasing a public performance license. If time or funds do not allow for this, searching for films within the public domain is the safest bet. Some of the films purchased by your media center or made for education audiences include a built-in license to allow for viewing beyond the scope of this exception and fair use. Always check into the licensing, and remember that copyright is always to be considered on a case-by-case basis.

I struggle with whether schools should purchase a public performance license to show films. A license certainly would be helpful for screening movies for entertainment purposes, enjoying films during school hours in any way beyond the scope of instruction, fundraisers, parent and student movie nights, and beyond. Although these cases require a public performance license, schools can also make the thoughtful decision to operate without them. The purposes requiring a license are all "extras." Focus specifically on learning. Go back to the heart of what you are trying to accomplish, which is doing what is best for student learning. Personally, I don't think showing a full film is the best decision for instruction in many situations. Although I have no data to support this, I wonder whether schools with a public performance license are more willing to allow the use of film, which, in turn, could have a negative impact on instruction. For example, if I teach a traditional schedule with seven periods in a day, I would probably need to take three class periods to watch an entire film with my students. Simply stated, educators can use their time with students more wisely.

If your school has cause to purchase a public performance license, you can turn to several places. Each licensing company has a variety of options; you might need to shop around a bit to find the license to best meet your needs. Companies offering public performance licenses work with different studios to represent them, and most offer licenses with K-12 public education in mind. In addition, these companies provide a great deal of copyright guidance and resources on their websites.

The Motion Picture Licensing Corporation (mplc.org) offers an umbrella license to simplify public performance licenses for schools and to allow schools to show films in any number of ways outside the scope of the Face-to-Face Teaching Exemption. Movie License USA (swank.com) is another great education-friendly public performance licensing company that gives flexible options such as an annual license, a single-event license, and even outdoor licensing.

If your school doesn't have a license, you may still find film to view on the public domain. I worked with a building principal at one point who wanted to help one of her school's clubs when the club members asked whether they could host a movie night at the school after hours for fun. They weren't sure what type of movie they could use for something like this, but they assumed they would be safe as long as they did not charge admission. They planned to sell concessions and use those proceeds as the fundraiser. The principal, a student leader, and I researched films within the public domain that the students might be excited to watch. We found that the 1960s film *Little Shop of Horrors* (what a great movie!) does not retain any type of copyright, as it is categorized as public domain, so this was suggested. I didn't attend the movie night, so I don't know whether they showed *Little Shop of Horrors* or not, but this process was a great opportunity to have conversations with educators and students about the protection of intellectual property and how we can do better once we slow down enough to act on what we know. Total transparency, however: there aren't that many films in the public domain that would work well for a movie night. Another suggestion to consider is to partner with an organization that does have a public performance license, which is the route one of our schools took to host an off-site event.

NETFLIX AND COPYRIGHT

In many school districts, Netflix is filtered for students and teachers while they are on campus. I am asked to explain why this is. Educators want to know whether they can log in to their Netflix accounts and show a film or program to their students. It makes sense that they would want to leverage such a powerful collection of resources for classroom use. I am reminded of hearing a pastor say, "Anything happening around me might end up in a sermon." Educators can say essentially the same thing: anything they come across might end up being used in their classrooms. While browsing Netflix at home, I can easily think of so many ways to weave these films into my class. In the case of Netflix, though, it seems your best option is to find another way. Netflix's Terms of Service explicitly state their "service and any content viewed through [their] service are for your personal and noncommercial use only and may not be shared with individuals beyond your household."[2]

When you examine the terms of use, which trump copyright law, or Terms of Service for web streaming tools, you are likely to find a similar message. I hope educators look to their technology departments as a layer of protection from violating these terms so teachers can focus on what really matters. Netflix does provide a specific list of documentaries they give permission for educators to show as part of classroom use. Be careful, however: there are a ton of resources out there that provide ideas for how to use Netflix films in class, but many of these do not take the terms of use into account. Netflix is the authority, so be sure to check out this list. This article published by Manchester University gives more specific details on popular streaming services: bit.ly/copyrighteousvideouse.

I HOPE EDUCATORS LOOK TO THEIR TECHNOLOGY DEPARTMENTS AS A LAYER OF PROTECTION FROM VIOLATING THESE TERMS SO TEACHERS CAN FOCUS ON WHAT REALLY MATTERS.

When educators choose to show an entire movie in class, they use what I call the "compare and contrast" excuse. As a former high school English teacher, I "may have" relied on this rationale occasionally. As a high school student, the only time I remember taking a similar assignment seriously was during a film literature class, and even then, only small clips of the film were truly analyzed. It may be easy for educators to say they should show only a shorter clip of a movie, but how can they do this intentionally? Consider the suggestions below for effectively using shorter film clips. (And by the way, showing clips of a movie in sequence is still showing the entire film. I see you, you loophole lovers!)

- Focus on a short clip and design a specific active learning opportunity focusing more time on thinking about the what and why for students than focusing on the clip itself.
- Ask students to choose a clip to view and ask them to justify how they want to use it to create or analyze.
- Choose a clip as a response to the previous day's discussion. Do students feel strongly about a topic? Find a clip challenging their assumptions or that will help them reflect on their position.
- Choose a clip from a film that inaccurately displays something from history and ask your students to examine it with a critical eye.
- Choose a clip and ask students to find evidence of bias.
- Choose a clip showing an important part of the plot of a story and ask students to justify or dispute the producer's choices based on evidence from their text.

WHAT ABOUT YOUTUBE?

As I write this, I am sitting on the couch in our living room. My two children, McKenna and Ryker, are following along with a YouTube video from the channel Art for Kids Hub on Kids YouTube. It is teaching them how to draw a fantastically iced birthday cake. They are sitting on the floor in front of the TV, surrounded by the perfect chaos of sketch paper and markers, pausing the video periodically to complete a new task with their creations. They aren't doing this for an assignment or because anyone told them to or even suggested that they do this. Instead, they stumbled on a tutorial on Kids YouTube and took the initiative on their own. In full disclosure, we are on day three of a cold/snow day school cancellation (thank you, Midwest living). They have been doing this for far longer than they normally do other tasks, as their ages would indicate.

Talking about the power of YouTube has become almost cliché for us in edtech. But it is so powerful. Truly, it can support our students in their own curiosity, exploration, and skill building in tremendous ways. It has become cliché to talk about it because its power is real.

Teachers across the globe have also responded to what a powerful classroom resource YouTube can be. I think it is safe to say that most of today's classrooms turn to YouTube as a resource for dynamic video content. If educators are regularly using YouTube in their classrooms, though, what should they consider when they filter it through the lens of copyright and responsible use? What should they consider when they use it as a way to share content they create personally or with their students? How can their use of YouTube become an opportunity for conversations with their students about copyright and respect for their own and others' intellectual property?

To start answering these questions, you should view and use content you find on YouTube in the same way you view and use content found elsewhere. Remember, terms of use trump copyright law. As a user of YouTube content, the YouTube terms of use state:

> *Content is provided to you AS IS. You may access Content for your information and personal use solely as intended through the provided functionality of the Service and as permitted under these Terms of Service. You shall not download any Content unless you see a "download" or similar link displayed by YouTube on the Service for that Content. You shall not copy, reproduce, distribute, transmit, broadcast, display, sell, license, or otherwise exploit any Content for any other purposes without the prior written consent of YouTube or the respective licensors of the Content. YouTube and its licensors reserve all rights not expressly granted in and to the Service and the Content.[3]*

As I interpret this as an educator, I draw the conclusion that we should feel free to use the videos by linking them in your content or directing your students to the YouTube video directly on the site, embedded in a Google Slides presentation, etc. The terms explicitly state that you should not download videos, retain copies, or remix unless permission is given. YouTube states that content is "provided to us as is," so you should use it as is. My ear to the ground tells me this is the use case for most of your classroom YouTube use.

Although you will see Creative Commons licenses applied to some You-Tube videos, the terms of use state that users cannot download content, which does not lend itself to remixing of any kind.

If you do want to search for videos with CC licenses to arm yourself with more information to help be sure you should be using the video in class, you can. When performing a search on YouTube, you can simply add a comma and creative commons (",creativecommons") to filter for videos marked with a license. A search for giraffes would look like "giraffes,creativecommons."

You also can filter after your search is complete by clicking the filter button and choosing the Creative Commons feature. This is a great tool for locating openly licensed content, but additional permission would have to be given for you to download.

THE FACT THAT IT IS AVAILABLE DOESN'T MAKE USING IT THE RIGHT DECISION.

• • • • • • • • • • •

Just like any source, you can never simply assume that because it is available you should be using it in class. Let's go back to our web filter example. Filtering the Internet is not a perfect science, and in turn, students can probably access things you might not want them to, even when a robust filter is applied. So, it is more important for educators to teach the skills so that students can self-regulate and make those decisions without our constant guidance. Similarly, YouTube has an insane amount of content available to use that you probably shouldn't be using. If you find an entire movie or an episode of a show on YouTube, odds are that the uploader is infringing. And if you choose to show something that you know is in violation, you are infringing just the same. The fact that it is available doesn't make using it the right decision.

YOUTUBE AS A CREATOR

I have heard educators essentially say, "YouTube is one big copyright violation." While this may be the perception of some, it is certainly not the message or the goal of YouTube. YouTube's Terms of Service clearly state for content creators:

YouTube does not endorse any Content submitted to the Service by any user or other licensor, or any opinion, recommendation, or advice expressed therein, and YouTube expressly disclaims any and all liability in connection with Content. YouTube does not permit copyright infringing activities and infringement of intellectual property rights on the Service, and YouTube will remove all Content if properly notified that such Content infringes on another's intellectual property rights. YouTube reserves the right to remove Content without prior notice.[4]

The resources found on YouTube (and other similar platforms) are unique because the provider itself (YouTube) is not actually responsible for the creation of the content.

In 1998, The Digital Millennium Copyright Act was signed in an effort to update copyright law in response to people's increased interaction with online resources. Specific to this discussion on YouTube, Title II of this Act explains its goal "to create four new limitations on liability for copyright infringement by online service providers."[5] Because of this Act, YouTube itself is not responsible for copyright infringements committed by content creators and sharers. However, YouTube does share resources to educate and help guide users and provides a process for handling claims of infringement. YouTube is a platform for video sharing, not a creator of content itself. If you come across a violation of copyright on YouTube, this falls on the video creator specifically, not on YouTube. While individuals can't control what is uploaded to YouTube, they can control what they use, how they use it, and the content they upload personally.

As I've said before, when you are a creator and sharer of content, you need to be sure the content you share is sound in a number of things, one being copyright. When you publish this content in such a widely used space, you are naturally more aware of it. Sharing your content adds an additional layer, and when you decide to do this, you open yourself up in a way, making you more vulnerable. This vulnerability gives you an opportunity to grow—specifically as a content sharer who considers existing content you are using as part of your own creations.

Beyond a foundational understanding of fair use, YouTube requires very specific terms of its creators. As a content creator using YouTube as a platform for sharing, YouTube terms clarify:

- You are responsible for being sure you are responsibly sharing and have permission to do so.
- You maintain ownership of your content.
- You agree to allow YouTube to use and redistribute.
- You agree to allow other users of YouTube access to your content.

YouTube is the perfect example of the power of sharing your creations. This power, combined with YouTube's excellent guidance on copyright and fair use, is probably the best path to take to help your students understand the importance of these skills and concepts. I will push back against those who view YouTube as a copyright violation nightmare and instead choose to see it as a most powerful tool to help others understand why this topic is central to so much of what educators do.

CHAPTER 15
Music

You never know what your students will hold on to and associate you with. For example, when I was in high school, one of my teachers loved the Pittsburgh Steelers. Although I am sure he really did love the Steelers, according to his students, they were pretty much foundational to his identity! In my fourth year of teaching, somehow Justin Bieber became what my students associated with me (facepalm!).

I was doing a mini lesson on pronoun–antecedent agreement, and while listening to a certain Bieber song, I noticed he used a lot of pronouns. In that moment, a lesson was born. In class, we listened to the song and evaluated his use of pronouns for clear antecedents and agreement. It was silly and fun and a less formal approach to a grammar mini lesson. My students, however, translated the lesson into "MRS. GILL LOVES THE BEEBS!" During the year, they gifted me with posters, stickers, trading cards—you name it—all the Justin Bieber fan merch anyone could ever need. I put the poster up in my room, and just enjoyed the fun of it. It became obvious very quickly that the lesson had run its course. Eventually, the class talked me into taking the poster down!

To be fair, this was right smack in the middle of the birth of the Beliebers—so don't judge me too harshly. As a music lover, I've found tons of ways to integrate it into the classroom. From listening to music as we wrote to encouraging its use in student projects, music has always been part of the classroom experiences I helped create. As I've learned and have grown as an educator, this is one practice I have reflected on. As the medium your students use to access music for their own enjoyment changes, you again have another opportunity to respond with some dialogue on creative property.

"THE LIMIT DOES NOT EXIST!"

A specific myth most educators have heard is, "we can use up to thirty seconds of a song however we would like to" without violating copyright. We have already established that no number rules exist to help us out here. Consider this influential quote to help you remember:

I did not choose this quote to suggest there are no limitations, but to reinforce that there are no concrete limitations. Copyright rules are complex and cannot rely on simple numbers as a way to simplify. Copyright as applied to music is a bit more complex because it splits into two parts. The recording of the music is copyright protected, and the musical composition is protected separately.

"THE LIMIT DOES NOT EXIST!"
—CADY HERON IN MEAN GIRLS

. . . .

If you feel it is necessary to use music in your materials or in student projects, you have to apply fair use and ask yourself which is best to consider in your particular use case. You must ask yourself the right questions:

- How are you using it?
- What parts are you using?
- Does it impact potential royalties?
- What is the nature of the work itself?

In addition, you have to be sure to inquire about reproducing, copying, and redistributing as well. And don't forget that terms of use trumps copyright law. With music, I suggest you err on the side of caution. If your students are looking to use clips of music as an element in a video project, I would use the opportunity to integrate a conversation about intellectual property and share platforms to search for royalty-free music. One of my very favorite student creation programs, WeVideo, includes hundreds of thousands of pieces of royalty-free content, including music and sound effects, that students can use to create engaging videos, right within the tool itself.

WITH MUSIC, I SUGGEST YOU ERR
ON THE SIDE OF CAUTION.
· · · · · · · · · · ·

In most cases, the way you ask students to use music in their creations probably would not be found as fair use. If you hope to enjoy background music in class, check the Terms of Service of the streaming product you have in mind. If you have an idea to incorporate music into your classroom beyond this, your music, band, or choir teachers may be (I hope!) the best resources and will know how to help you determine what you can make copies of, what you can perform, etc.

Boy, does this bring back memories from my first couple of years teaching! Raise your hand if you ever had your students do the "soundtrack" project. Honestly, the project itself doesn't turn my stomach; the way I implemented it does. Students were to choose songs to create a soundtrack to accompany the plot of a novel they read. They chose important parts of the plot, discussed the characters, pulled quotes from the story, and analyzed what impacted the mood and tone. They designed a cover (back in the CD days) and then—they burned the music onto a CD to bring into class to play. The students who chose to create this product were then left to figure out where to get their music and how to burn it onto the CD. Napster was pretty well dead by this time, but I have no clue what process the students used to get their music. What I do know is I missed a huge opportunity to help them make the best decisions for this.

Copyright protection is broad where music is concerned. Covering a song? You have to consider copyright. Lip dub? You have to consider copyright. If fair use doesn't apply, you need permission, unless the licensing of the work already allows for your use. YouTube has become a platform to both share and enjoy music, too, and YouTube encourages artistic expression while supporting copyright through their Share the Revenue agreement. This encourages performers to cover songs from a specific list and potentially monetize their channels while increasing their own reach.[1]

The YouTube Copyright Center has a ton of resources if you are looking to dig a bit deeper, and the YouTube Creator Academy has online courses, lessons, and quizzes, some focusing specifically on copyright. If you add content to a YouTube channel at any level, I would encourage you to check out these resources with your students. Some of my favorite places to get openly licensed or royalty-free music to use as part of student video projects include:

- YouTube Audio Library
- Bensound.com
- Free Music Archive
- Jamendo

Remember to follow the Creative Commons license if you are using an openly licensed song. Follow the best practices for attribution and be sure you are allowed to modify the song if you plan on cutting it to use as part of something new.

The soundtrack assignment has an update I would love to share!

CHAPTER 16
Beg, Borrow, and Steal from Students?

In 2015 Anthony Mazur, a sophomore high school student in Texas, began selling on his personal Flickr account the pictures he was taking for the student yearbook. During his time as a journalism student, he had attended a conference and heard a speaker share how he sold the images he took to local newspapers. Mazur thought this was a good idea, so he started submitting his photos to parents and newspapers. When the school found out about it, he was called into the office. The school argued that Mazur violated student privacy rights by posting the images, and the administration eventually asked him to sign a directive stating he would take the photos down from his site. Even though a school policy stated that students retain the rights to their creative content even when the content is created for school using school equipment, the school maintained that the images were the property of the school. As the school pressed Mazur on this issue, people rallied to support him in his right to retain ownership of his photographs. The hashtag #IAmAnthony grew to support him and all things related to student rights and free press.

In June of 2018,[1] Mazur dropped the lawsuit after a three-year fight in response to the school agreeing to honor his rights to his photographs. The school also agreed that students were no longer required to sign any sort of document in relation to the ownership of their work.

Although educators know that work for hire applies to them, regardless of whether it is specifically outlined in their teacher contract, they also must consider this from the lens of a student. Students maintain ownership of the work they create. Even though they are earning a grade and credit for a course they complete, the work they create is theirs. Work for hire simply does not apply to students.

Educators often hear the phrase "student ownership." Or they hear someone speak of student engagement by using the phrase "taking ownership of their education." These phrases usually refer to a student's involvement in the learning process, but literal ownership of student work is a topic educators need to understand. The bottom line is that students do maintain ownership of what they create. This raises a few questions in my mind:

- Do students want the items they create? If they are simply responding to questions they Googled as part of a worksheet, probably not.
- What type of opportunities are teachers giving students?
- Are they inspiring students to create something they would be willing to fight to keep?

=====

#IAmAnthony
-ANTHONY MAZUR-

I was very curious about Anthony's story, so I reached out to him to see whether he would be willing to tell me about it. He was gracious and willing, and we spoke on the phone for about an hour. He had a lot to say. In our conversation, I asked him whether he could help me identify why copyright isn't always a priority in K-12 education. His response?

> *"We simply aren't afraid of getting caught. You can tell people all you want it is wrong or illegal. But if they have this mentality, it is really hard. They would understand if something similar happened to them. But if they aren't producing content, they don't understand the importance of protecting copyright. It is so widespread and the law has become so murky—but [violations are] so common. The copyright laws weren't written with the modern Internet in mind."*

Anthony moved on to talk about film as an example.

> *"'Piracy is not a victimless crime,' We ignore this FBI warning at the beginning of a movie. Are people aware of this, or do they just not care? Honestly, I'm not sure I have a good answer. If they don't care, they don't*

care. It should go beyond training teachers on copyright. People need to be more aware of being virtuous online citizens. It is a sign we are in troubled times already if the response is 'I don't care because I'm not going to get caught even though I know what I'm doing is wrong.'"

After sharing his story of conflict and creative property, Anthony argued that schools should be doing more to encourage entrepreneurship in students.

"They should create a course on how to run a small business. This would have been the proper thing to do. We had a large district, and they could have offered a class specifically tailored to helping kids with talent to develop their talent and run a small business. This would have been a win-win. Schools have to champion for their students and these types of classes and educate them to be successful entrepreneurs."

As we chatted about the misunderstanding of work for hire and how it relates to students, we considered whether today's students care enough about the work they do in school to actually fight to protect their ownership of it as he did.

"Obviously schools have the power. Teachers are adults and can willingly enter into contracts, but this doesn't mean we have to say that schools own everything in totality. I was the only photographer dedicated to taking photos in all the schools. I liked it and it was fun, and if I knew parents might want to buy these, it gave me incentive to work. In a similar way to teachers, schools can maintain ownership. What if a journalism teacher writes a really good article? How can we incentivize both students and teachers to take ownership and care about the work they create? How does encouraging the protection of creative property in kindergarten through twelfth-grade environments provide this incentive?"

ENCOURAGING STUDENT CREATIVITY: LET YOUR STUDENTS SING

If educators want to encourage students to be creative and take ownership of their work, they must clearly communicate to ensure students that the work they are producing truly will be theirs. But how can educators do this?

Ask students to create from a spirit of authenticity. The first time I tried project-based learning (PBL) in my class, it was sort of a disaster. My students weren't accustomed to working in a PBL environment, and I didn't have any formal training on PBL at the time. But I wanted to try something to give them an opportunity to create a product they felt mattered. The prompt of the project asked students to work on something as a way to give back to the school or the community. Granted, this was years ago, and I wouldn't approach the unit the same way now, but it was quickly clear they were confused. They wanted to be told exactly what to do. The project had the right spirit, but I was attempting to take the students through a quick process of asking them to forget about my expectations and how many points things were worth, and simply try to make a difference in our school. Most educators recognize the power authentic learning can have in their classrooms, and PBL can give them a structure to sharpen their students into humans who see themselves not only as students, but as members of their communities who are able to bring about change right now. Educators can empower students to problem solve today.

Avoid projects resulting in thirty identical products. If you are asking students to stick to a project script, what are you really asking of them? How can you modify it so students aren't always forced to fit the mold? How creative can students really get if you are directing every decision—what to put where, etc.? The end result might look creative, but what would students accomplish if we let go of that control? Really, is this sort of project engaging students in active learning? Is it anything more than a nice-looking worksheet? Maybe not.

Encourage students to go beyond the options you give them. Tell me if you have experienced this: I would give students a project (think dessert projects for this example, not project-based learning), and I would give a list of ways they could create. I would provide three to six options (do this or this or this), and the very last bullet point would say something like: if you have another idea, run it by me! I honestly don't remember one single student taking me up on that creative freedom option, ever, in my entire career. They had been so used to being told what to do, so when presented with a list of options, choosing one that had already been fleshed out seemed like the safest bet. I had more success when I didn't give any options at all and had the students design from scratch, but it wasn't something that came without a ton of support.

Be thoughtful about the use of templates and examples. I have gone back and forth about using templates and examples my entire teaching career. Currently, I am on the side of not using them when possible. As a younger teacher, I thought it was important to show my students exactly what I expected, and showing examples was the best way I knew to do this, especially when it came to larger projects. My fear with this practice, though, is that some students don't go beyond what the example shows, or worse, they put their energy into recreating what they saw. This is another example of students being great at "doing school." The same thing goes for templates. I still use templates—when it makes sense. Sometimes you have to prioritize the skills you are assessing and focusing on. For example, if you are asking students to create an infographic, but you want to focus on research skills, maybe it makes sense to give students a template to plug their research into. However, if you want to support them in organizing information and graphic design and jump into a conversation about the balance between high-quality content and high-quality design, then not using a template is likely preferable so that students have the space and the opportunity to learn all of those things. If the template or the example limits your students from growing, I say ditch it!

ENCOURAGE STUDENTS TO GO BEYOND THE OPTIONS YOU GIVE THEM.

Give them an audience other than you. When students create for a class—whether the product is a response to a prompt, an infographic, a paper, or something else you are asking them to create—typically, their audience for it is you and their fellow classmates. Educators understand students' word choice and tone are influenced by their audience. When you expand the audience that your students are creating for, the tone of their work can change, too. Bring in a panel of local business owners, university representatives, or public figures to give feedback on student work. Schools within my district take this approach in their project-based learning assessments during second semester, and it is an incredible experience for all involved. Find someone to connect with, using Skype or Google Hangouts, and set up expert chats for your students to participate in. Find a classroom in a different district, state, or country, and arrange for your students to have a virtual partner. Read a book along with another class and conduct a virtual book club. Encourage your students to publish and share in virtual spaces to extend the reach of their voice. Ask them who they would want to connect with, and graciously ask those individuals to participate. Again and again, I am humbled by the generosity of the world.

Encourage student PLNs. If you know that building a personal learning network is important for educators, why wouldn't you help your students leverage the same collaborative power? How might you help your students build a network to support their growth? Build in feedback groups that rotate throughout the year. Discuss how to give feedback, and give students opportunities to bounce ideas off of one another. How would learning change if you incorporated into every learning process working with another student—in your class, in another class or another school, or in college? Could you help students find local field experts to include in part of a relevant project? Support students in finding a local expert, assist them in contacting the experts in the community, and teach your students to advocate for themselves. Set up a day in which your students can meet with the experts during school hours to collaborate, and if that isn't possible, this is certainly a situation in which technology can assist.

Ask students for their ideas. Instead of building a list of ideas for students to choose from, why not start with a blank page and let students come up with the list? Start the conversation by sharing with students the skill or skills you'd like to focus on mastering, and brainstorm ways you can grow in this skill either as a whole group or in smaller groups. As you brainstorm together, let natural groups form based on interest and passion. Show your students you are invested in making learning authentic and personal to them by finding ways to let go of your control at times and let them take the lead.

Engage students in the design thinking process. Design thinking is a process for solving problems in a creative way. The design thinking process is an incredible opportunity you can give your students because it challenges them to think both critically and creatively. The first time I went through the design thinking process from start to finish, I was thirty-three. In all of my years as a student, educator, and lifelong learner, I had never been as frustrated with the learning process. I must admit I was near tears several times. I was working on a project, getting feedback, and feeling vulnerable. But I was also learning about myself and the project itself more than I would have if I had simply completed the project solo, submitted it, and received feedback. What is special about the design thinking process is that your facilitator doesn't always answer your questions directly but instead guides you to ask yourself the questions that move you toward growth. This is what ownership of learning is all about.

CHAPTER 17
Attribution

One of the biggest misconceptions educators have about using any digital content they find is that they are good to go—as long as they cite it. But this is not true. Educators who believe this have forgotten an important step in the process: how are they using the item, and do they have permission to use it in this way? Have they considered the four factors? Once they know they can use the item in the way they hope, they also need to consider what information should be included in a proper attribution.

WRITING A PROPER ATTRIBUTION

What information should you include? You need the title, the source, the author, and the license.

The title: What the resource is named.
The source: Where did it come from?
The author: Who published or created it?
The license: How does the creator want this used?

How do you locate this information? You have to get comfortable rooting around for the information sometimes, because each site organizes this information differently. You can also do what I do—generally stick to the same few sites when creating content to make locating these items quicker. Using platforms partnered with Creative Commons also makes this process easier. If not, you can generally find the licensing information by doing minimal investigation.

How do you include it in your work? Gather the information you need, hyperlink the heck out of it, and don't stress too much about the format.

"Best Practices for Attribution" is a page shared on wiki.creativecommons.org.[1] Because the page is licensed under a Creative Commons license, I can share its content with you here. Super cool! The CC-BY-4.0 International license is approved for free cultural works and allows for sharing and remixing of the content, even for commercial purposes. Check it out below, slightly adapted from the source! (And check out the attribution below the material!)

EXAMPLES OF ATTRIBUTION

Below this photo are some examples of how people might attribute it.

"Ideal" Attribution:
"Creative Commons 10th Birthday Celebration San Francisco" by tvol is licensed under CC BY 2.0
This is an ideal attribution because it contains all four pieces of required information in detail and includes links to most of the information.
Title: "Creative Commons 10th Birthday Celebration San Francisco"
Author: "tvol" (linked to the author's profile page)
Source: "Creative Commons 10th Birthday Celebration San Francisco" (linked to original Flickr page
License: "CC BY 2.0" (linked to license deed)

"Pretty Good" Attribution:

Photo by tvol / CC BY

This a "pretty good" attribution because it has most of the required information and provides links to some of it.

Title: Title is not noted (and it should be), but at least the source is linked.

Author: "tvol"

Source:"Photo" (linked to original Flickr page)

License: "CC BY" (linked to license deed)

"Incorrect" Attribution:

Photo: Creative Commons

This attribution is incorrect for several reasons.

Title: Title is not noted.

Author: Creative Commons is not the author of this photo.

Source: No link is provided to the original photo.

License: There is no mention of the license ("Creative Commons" is an organization), much less a link to the license.

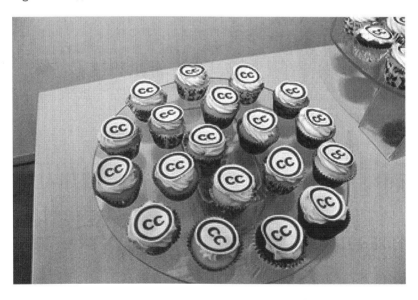

"Good" Attribution (for material you modified slightly):

"Creative Commons 10th Birthday Celebration San Francisco" by tvol, used under CC BY / Desaturated from original

This is a good attribution because it contains all four pieces of essential information, and an explanation of the modification is included.

Title, Author, Source, License: All are noted.

Modification: "Desaturated from original"

"Good" Attribution (material from which you created a derivative work):
This work, "90fied," is a derivative of "Creative Commons 10th Birthday Celebration San Francisco" by tvol, used under CC BY. "90fied" is licensed under CC BY by [Your name here].

This attribution is good because it contains all four required pieces of information as well as a note of explanation about the derivation.

Original Title, Author, Source, License: All are noted.

Derivative: "This work, '90fied,' is a derivative of..."

New author of the derivative work is also noted

Note: If you're at a point where you are licensing derivative works, go to: Marking your work with a CC license (wiki.creativecommons.org/wiki/Marking_your_work_with_a_CC_license).

The section below is also attributed to Best Practices for Attribution on wiki.creativecommones.org. (Attribution below.)

TASL

Title—What is the name of the material?
If a title was provided for the material, include it. Sometimes a title is not provided; in that case, don't worry about it.

Author—Who owns the material?
Name the author or authors of the material in question. Sometimes, the licensor may want you to give credit to some other entity, like a company or pseudonym. In rare cases, the licensor may not want to be attributed at all. In all of these cases, just do what they request.

Source —Where can I find it?
Since you somehow accessed the material, you know where to find it. Provide the source of the material so others can, too. Since we live in the age of the Internet, this is usually a URL or hyperlink where the material resides.

License—How can I use it?
You are obviously using the material for free thanks to the CC license, so make note of it. Don't just say the material is Creative Commons, because that says nothing about how the material can actually be used. Remember that there are six different CC licenses; which one is the material under? Name and provide a link to it, *e.g.,* http://creativecommons.org/licenses/by/4.0/ for CC BY.

If the licensor included a license notice with more information, include that as well.

DON'T MAKE IT ANY MORE COMPLICATED THAN IT IS—JUST PASS ON ANY INFO YOU THINK IS IMPORTANT.

Lastly, is there anything else I should know before I use it?
When you accessed the material originally, did it come with any copyright notices, a notice that refers to the disclaimer of warranties, or a notice of previous modifications? (That was a mouthful!) Because that kind of legal mumbo jumbo is actually pretty important to potential users of the material. So best practice is to just retain all of that stuff by copying and

pasting such notices into your attribution. Don't make it any more complicated than it is—just pass on any info you think is important.

Attribution of the attribution content above: It's an inception attribution!

HAT TIP

One of the easiest and most visible ways to give credit to someone for an idea or creation is through the use of a hat tip. Although this is not a literal tipping of the hat to someone, it is a *thank you* from across the room—or across a Tweet, if you will. The gesture of a hat tip is meant to acknowledge someone, and this connected version allows you to do this.

Consider this scenario: you come across a thread on Twitter in which a few educators are looking for a resource on a specific topic. You have just the thing! When Tweeting back to the thread with a link to the resource you have in mind, you also take a moment to tag the person who created and shared the resource with you initially. Your Tweet might look like this:

Try this out! H/T to @someoneawesome for creating and sharing this with me! Check it out!

The person you tag and thank is reminded of why sharing is so important. You've also helped people connect, and you never know where the connection might lead. Additionally, you've modeled for your followers the practice of giving a shoutout to those who share with you while respecting their intellectual and creative property. All of this goes a long way toward building and sustaining a culture of sharing, especially if those around you pick it up and add it to their practice as well.

H/T to @micheeaton (Michele Eaton) for teaching me about the H/T!

CHAPTER 18
Model

As an educator, provide attributions in all you create. It's important.

As an English teacher, in terms of content, I was most passionate about teaching students to write. One of the courses I taught was Advanced Composition, a dual-credit, semester-long course for senior students. One of my favorite components of the class was to supporting students as they let their research guide the topics they wrote about. Instead of choosing a topic out of thin air, I encouraged them to start by researching topics they were interested in or curious about, and then let their research move them down a path of discovery. I challenged them to use the essays as an opportunity to create something new—a new perspective, comparison, or idea. I made a huge deal out of this. Another teacher challenged me, saying new ideas don't exist. While I understand the point she was making, I still maintain that every person has the ability to put their own spin on something, and a fresh perspective on a topic is what makes it "new."

Another piece of this course taught students the difference between direct quotations in academic writing and paraphrasing research. The process of inserting each into an essay is different, although both require in-text citations. Inevitably, at least one student would become frustrated and wonder how she could possibly differentiate what part of the paper was her own interpretation and analysis of research and how much of it was something she had learned somewhere else. I find myself caught in this strange web, too. I'll call it the pressure to over-attribute. If I care about copyright, how far do I go?

ONE WAY YOU CAN MAKE IMMEDIATE CHANGES IS TO START VISIBLY ATTRIBUTING THINGS YOU USE IN YOUR CONTENT.

. . . .

One way you can make immediate changes is to start visibly attributing things you use in your content. When I had the copyright epiphany, I knew even if I wasn't talking about copyright issues with students or other educators, my content at least had a Creative Commons license on it. In earlier days, though I wouldn't point it out, I at least put "Created by Diana Gill" at the bottom. I was visibly taking action on showing the importance of ownership. Every once in a while, someone asked about it, and I took advantage of the opportunity—trying to keep it cute, play it cool, and not get too excited! When I used an image within the public domain or something licensed CC0, I still provided an attribution to keep it visible. It felt like a simple, tangible change I could make. Rushton Hurley is a great example of a well-known speaker who is intentional about this; when he gives a keynote address, each slide includes an image with a tiny Creative Commons attribution at the bottom.

LICENSE YOUR CREATIONS AND REMIXES

When you create something from scratch, a new product using openly licensed material, or an activity considering fair use when pulling from other sources, add a final layer to your publishing, regardless of what publishing means to you in each situation. If you create something for use in your class, add a Creative Commons license before you share it. If you add a newly created hyperdoc to the Teachers Give Teachers movement, add a Creative Commons license before uploading to the platform (instructions to follow). If you create any sort of visual media, add Creative Commons license metadata information when you share it out on platforms collaborating with Creative Commons. Consider choosing the platforms you share on based on the list of platforms recognizing the Creative Commons licenses. If you create a Slides presentation to be used as part of a PD workshop you are leading, add a Creative Commons license to the last slide and share it with others who could benefit from seeing or using the resource. If you are proud of it and believe others could benefit from using your work, or if someone asks you for a resource you wouldn't mind sharing, slap a license on that baby before you send it off. This added step honors your work as a creator and lets you have a specific say in how your materials are used. It also keeps you on point with how you are using resources within the work you create and models for everyone the protection of intellectual property. Finally, it encourages a culture of sharing to support growth in all parts of the educational process. If one person asks you about the licenses they see, you can open the door to conversation and encourage them to license the work they create, too.

SLAP A LICENSE ON IT!

After you create something you want to use in your classroom, share with your colleagues, or share with the world, consider how you want the resource to be used after it leaves your hands. If you are sharing, you want other people to benefit from its use, right?

Keep in mind, the type of resource you created should dictate the type of license you want to use. Remember also that your creation has been copyright protected since its conception—the licenses are simply allowing you to control the little pieces of it in a manageable way. The topic and the type of resource should guide your responses to these questions. Avoid getting into the habit of simply picking your favorite license and using it in all situations.

Head to creativecommons.org/share-your-work to digitally start this process. Be ready to answer the following questions as you select the perfect license for your creation.

Do you want your work to be adapted in any way? If your creation is something you see as useful in the classroom, it most likely makes sense for teachers to be able to modify it to meet the unique needs or their students. On the other hand, if changes could negatively impact what you've created, you might answer no to this first question. For example, when I create a PD course or a presentation on copyright, I might decide it is best if the resource is used but not adapted in any way.

Do you want others to be able to financially benefit from using your work? I usually choose not to allow this, and I'll be a bit persuasive on this one. As an educator, you have to assume those most likely to benefit from the work you are sharing are also educators. And, to hint back to a major point in this overall message, educators have to have each other's backs.

I don't want someone charging an educator for something I created for classroom use. Are you making money off of the creation of your work? This is something to consider when making this decision. Reflect back on our conversation about work for hire, and consider those who have found the work they have created and shared freely uploaded to platforms by someone else for financial gain.

Do you want recognition for the work you did? Luckily, the Creative Commons licenses make this one a no-brainer. All of the licenses, with the exception of CC0, require attribution be made. If you want to release your work for use and do not feel it is necessary to require attribution, you can certainly consider a CC0 license. Creative Commons provides guidance and resources either to license your work under CC0 or to add a public domain mark to your work.

You also need to consider whether you want to add the SA addition to your license. SA stands for "share alike," and it requires the person using a modification or a remix of your work to license their new remix in the same way, in an effort to keep the ripple moving through the water. Essentially the SA says, "I'll share mine; I just ask you also share yours."

Will you be sharing your work on a platform allowing you to make use of the machine-readable metadata by using the HTML code? If so, fill out the section on the form as you build your license. You will have to provide the title of your work, the name you would like your work attributed to, and any appropriate URLs.

After going through the process and selecting the features of the license you would like to use, you can simply copy and paste the license information. In some cases, it will make sense to copy and paste the license image and license text to insert them into your work. This is the method I choose if I am adding the license to a Google Doc or resource created using Google Slides. However, if you are uploading to a different platform able to make use of the embed code or want to use it within your website, you can also copy and paste the code Creative Commons provides as a result of your going through the process of selecting the license you want to apply to your work. This process is great because it is incredibly user friendly for you as well. Not only can you copy and paste the license information, but the necessary text will be hyperlinked so a user can read more about the licensing terms you have chosen.

I also love the Google Docs add-on for choosing and applying a license if you are working within this system. This is great for all the hyperdoc lovers out there. To get the add-on:

- Open up a Google Doc
- Select Add-ons
- Choose Get Add-ons

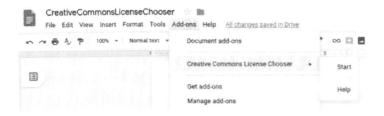

- Search for Creative Commons. You will see the Creative Commons license chooser pop up in your search results.
- Click the Add button to add it within your Google account. As of right now, this tool is only available within Google Docs, but I hope it becomes available within other GSuite tools as well.
- When you are ready to use the tool to apply a license to your Doc, click Add-ons and start the Creative Commons License chooser.
- A dashboard will open up on the right of your Google Doc. It will walk you through responses to two questions to help you determine which license should be added to your Doc.
- From there, all you have to do is click "Insert License information into this document," and the license information will pop into the document at your cursor's current location.

So let's be honest here. Who is to say that if you add a license to your work, everyone with access to your work (once you share it out, it is difficult to control) will abide by the license features and terms that you choose? You simply can't control that—in the same way that you can't control but only work and hope to influence anything. But it is more powerful to empower each other to share instead of holding ourselves back from sharing just because we let that concern impact our decisions.

BUT IT IS MORE POWERFUL TO EMPOWER EACH OTHER TO SHARE INSTEAD OF HOLDING OURSELVES BACK FROM SHARING JUST BECAUSE WE LET THAT CONCERN IMPACT OUR DECISIONS.

. . . .

POINT TO RESOURCES

Point educators and students to resources that support sharing and proper attribution.

As you shift toward more focus on copyright and attribution, tackle one thing at a time. I've made the mistake of grading a paper with a red pen and literally marking every single thing I could find. Grammar mistake? Red mark. Parallel structure issue? Red mark. Content feedback? Red feedback. In my head, I thought I needed to show I read every word and put tons of effort into grading, since my students had put a ton of work into writing the paper. That was fair, right? Wrong. All I did was give feedback rarely used—or even read—by the student. I likely I ended up doing more harm to the students by offending them with an overwhelming sense of "I did all of that wrong?!" (Okay, I didn't actually use red pen, but it doesn't matter.)

Gradually, I began to realize that if I just focused on helping the student improve the most important skills, I saw more growth. It wasn't about quantity—but quality. I like to take the same approach with all things copyright, too. Tearing apart everything you do, use, and create all at once is a recipe for disaster. Instead, choose one thing at a time to focus on.

Become best friends with your media specialist. I am not being dramatic when I say media specialists are the unsung heroes of your schools. As a classroom teacher, my media specialist was a beacon of guiding light (and continues to be because I still ask her questions weekly). For co-teaching, brainstorming, student support, project ideas—you name it—my media specialist was my go-to.

The scope of educators' jobs has grown exponentially. When you think about all of the chaos you attempt to calm on a daily basis, it is a pretty extensive list. And, of course, all of this is in addition to the skills you want to lead your students to master. One recent and big change in education is the shift to digital resources and technology-enhanced instruction. All of this is beyond powerful, but it brings with it some real challenges. Maybe challenge is too strong a word, but the terrain educators navigate isn't always level and easy. Two hills educators need to climb together are information literacy and digital citizenship, and the very best trail buddy they can have by their sides is their media specialist. You might fumble your way through learning to tie the strongest knots or have a great book about which wild berries to eat, but your media specialists are the trail guides; they know where to go and how to read the map. They have an internal compass, but they also keep a few spare compasses handy to share with others who are less comfortable. They teach you how to track and read the signs. They know what and who to trust. They are your best resource for navigating the places you need to explore.

And the point of this thinly veiled metaphor is to impress upon you with a little flair the fact that your media specialist was born to support the work you do with information literacy and beyond. So let them do their thing.

Shoutout to all of the media specialists out there. You guys are the real deal! Janna Carney Moran, thanks for being my lifeboat and helping me become info lit! And if you work in a school without a media specialist currently, head to my website and find a letter to use to start your campaign for one!

TEARING APART EVERYTHING YOU DO, USE, AND CREATE ALL AT ONCE IS A RECIPE FOR DISASTER. INSTEAD, CHOOSE ONE THING AT A TIME TO FOCUS ON.

- - - - - - - - - - -

KEEP FIGHTING ▲ THE GOOD FIGHT

One of the first times I started to take actionable steps toward improving the culture of copyright and the support educators received in relation to this was for a breakout session at our state's ISTE affiliate conference. I titled the session "Copyright Coaching" and focused on ways that technology and instructional coaches could and should help lead the charge in supporting teachers. I discussed the best approaches to take, how to fit it in, what to focus on, and where to start. It was big picture thinking at that point.

Near the end of the session, a fellow technology coach in my state asked me what I would do if people hearing this message just refused to care about it at all. The answer I gave that day remains the same. It's also the advice I would give to coaches who are working with technology-reluctant educators or educators who live with a fixed mindset and haven't put a lot of headspace into being reflective: We have to keep on fighting the good fight.

Just like with the use of technology in education, we know that not everyone has bought in. So that doesn't mean we just give up; we work with those who are eager to learn and grow, and we let the fire of that build and build until everyone wants to be part of it. In terms of copyright and all things related, we keep spreading that message, because ultimately, it isn't about doing things right or wrong. It's about knowing better and doing better. It's about encouraging a culture of sharing. It's about understanding how to appropriately use resources and protect the intellectual property of others. It's about seeing yourself as a creator. It's about doing better once you know what better looks like. It's about expanding our knowledge of this to be prepared to help our students out in this age of constant access. It's about being able to provide our students every skill they need to consider themselves creators as well. So although we know that not everyone will be on board right away, or even if we think that we will never get buy-in from one hundred percent of the educators that we know, we have to try to do the right thing and support our educational and creative process in this way.

BIBLIOGRAPHY

CHAPTER 5

1, 2. "Children's Internet Protection Act (CIPA). *Federal Communications Commission*. https://www.fcc.gov/consumers/guides/childrens-Internet-protection-act.
3. "Office of Non-Public Education (ONPE). *U.S. Department of Education*. https://www2.ed.gov/about/offices/list/oii/nonpublic/erate.html.

CHAPTER 6

1. "Defining the "Open" in Open Content and Open Educational Resources." http://opencontent.org/definition/.

CHAPTER 7

1, 2. "Welcome to #GoOpen." *Office of Educational Technology*. https://tech.ed.gov/open/districts/launch/welcome/.
3. "More Information on Fair Use." *United States Copyright Office*. https://www.copyright.gov/fair-use/more-info.html
4. "Definitions." *United States Copyright Office*. https://www.copyright.gov/help/faq-definitions.html.
5. "Duration of Copyright." *United States Copyright Office*. https://www.copyright.gov/circs/circ15a.pdf.

CHAPTER 12

1. "Copyright in General." *United States Copyright Office*. https://www.copyright.gov/help/faq/faq-general.html.
2. "The 18th Century." *United States Copyright Office*. https://www.copyright.gov/timeline/timeline_18th_century.html.
3, 4. "1950 – 1997." *United States Copyright Office*. https://www.copyright.gov/timeline/timeline_1950-1997.html.

5. "Copyright Basics." *United States Copyright Office.*
https://www.copyright.gov/circs/circ01.pdf
6. "The Digital Millennium Copyright Act of 1998." *United States Copyright Office.* https://www.copyright.gov/legislation/dmca.pdf.

CHAPTER 13

1. "Best Practices for Attribution." *Creative Commons Wiki.*
https://wiki.creativecommons.org/wiki/best_practices_for_attribution.

CHAPTER 14

1. "Circular 92 Copyright Law of the United States and Related Laws Contained in Title 17 of the United States Code." *United States Copyright Office.* copyright.gov/title17/title17.pdf.
2. "Netflix Terms of Use." *Netflix.* Last modified April 24, 2019.
help.netflix.com/legal/termsofuse.
3, 4. "Terms of Service." *YouTube.* Last modified May 25, 2018.
https://www.youtube.com/t/terms.
5. "The Digital Millennium Copyright Act of 1998." *United States Copyright Office.* https://www.copyright.gov/legislation/dmca.pdf.

CHAPTER 15

1. "Monetizing Eligible Cover Videos." *YouTube.*
https://support.google.com/youtube/answer/3301938.

CHAPTER 16

1. "After Three Years, Anthony Mazur Wins Ownership of His Photos and His Former High School Has Promised to Stop Making StudentsSign over Their Copyright." *Student Press Law Center.* splc.org/article/2018/03/anthony-mazur-lawsuit.

CHAPTER 17

1. "Best Practices for Attribution." *Creative Commons Wiki.*
https://wiki.creativecommons.org/wiki/best_practices_for_attribution.

BRING DIANA GILL TO YOUR SCHOOL OR DISTRICT

KEYNOTE AND SESSION TOPICS

- Licensed to GILL—Learn about how to properly attribute content and license your creative content, plus, pass these skills on to your students.
- Integrating Copyright
- Information Literacy
- Digital Citizenship—Ideas to integrate digital citizenship into daily learning.
- OER—Searching for, vetting, and using open educational resources.
- Designing Digital Lessons
- Blended Learning
- In Yo' Face—Instructional Videos Featuring YOU!
- The subOS Update—How to design lessons for a substitute teacher to implement that help you make the most of instructional time.
- Google Level 1 and 2 Training
- A Storyboard for Professional Learning—How can you leverage your professional development time to best focus on your goals? Let's work together to come up with a plan.
- Video Editing: An Amateur's Guide

Webste: dianargill.com
Twitter: @dianargill

More from

Dave Burgess Consulting, Inc.

Since 2012, DBCI has been publishing books that inspire and equip educators to be their best. For more information on our DBCI titles or to purchase bulk orders for your school, district, or book study, visit DaveBurgessconsulting.com/DBCIbooks.

MORE FROM THE LIKE A PIRATE™ SERIES

- *Teach Like a PIRATE* by Dave Burgess
- *eXPlore Like a Pirate* by Michael Matera
- *Learn Like a Pirate* by Paul Solarz
- *Play Like a Pirate* by Quinn Rollins
- *Run Like a Pirate* by Adam Welcome

LEAD LIKE A PIRATE™ SERIES

- *Lead Like a PIRATE* by Shelley Burgess and Beth Houf
- *Balance Like a Pirate* by Jessica Cabeen, Jessica Johnson, and Sarah Johnson
- *Lead beyond Your Title* by Nili Bartley
- *Lead with Culture* by Jay Billy
- *Lead with Literacy* by Mandy Ellis

LEADERSHIP & SCHOOL CULTURE

- *Culturize* by Jimmy Casas
- *Escaping the School Leader's Dunk Tank* by Rebecca Coda and Rick Jetter
- *From Teacher to Leader* by Starr Sackstein

- *The Innovator's Mindset* by George Couros
- *Kids Deserve It!* by Todd Nesloney and Adam Welcome
- *Let Them Speak* by Rebecca Coda and Rick Jetter
- *The Limitless School* by Abe Hege and Adam Dovico
- *The Pepper Effect* by Sean Gaillard
- *The Principled Principal* by Jeffrey Zoul and Anthony McConnell
- *Relentless* by Hamish Brewer
- *The Secret Solution* by Todd Whitaker, Sam Miller, and Ryan Donlan
- *Start. Right. Now.* by Todd Whitaker, Jeffrey Zoul, and Jimmy Casas
- *Stop. Right. Now.* by Jimmy Casas and Jeffrey Zoul
- *They Call Me "Mr. De"* by Frank DeAngelis
- *Unmapped Potential* by Julie Hasson and Missy Lennard
- *Word Shift* by Joy Kirr
- *Your School Rocks* by Ryan McLane and Eric Lowe

TECHNOLOGY & TOOLS

- *50 Things You Can Do with Google Classroom* by Alice Keeler and Libbi Miller
- *50 Things to Go Further with Google Classroom* by Alice Keeler and Libbi Miller
- *140 Twitter Tips for Educators* by Brad Currie, Billy Krakower, and Scott Rocco
- *Block Breaker* by Brian Aspinall
- *Code Breaker* by Brian Aspinall
- *Google Apps for Littles* by Christine Pinto and Alice Keeler
- *Master the Media* by Julie Smith
- *Shake Up Learning* by Kasey Bell
- *Social LEADia* by Jennifer Casa-Todd
- *Teaching Math with Google Apps* by Alice Keeler and Diana Herrington
- *Teachingland* by Amanda Fox and Mary Ellen Weeks

TEACHING METHODS & MATERIALS

- *All 4s and 5s* by Andrew Sharos
- *Boredom Busters* by Katie Powell
- *The Classroom Chef* by John Stevens and Matt Vaudrey
- *Ditch That Homework* by Matt Miller and Alice Keeler
- *Ditch That Textbook* by Matt Miller
- *Don't Ditch That Tech* by Matt Miller, Nate Ridgway, and Angelia Ridgway
- *EDrenaline Rush* by John Meehan
- *Educated by Design* by Michael Cohen, The Tech Rabbi
- *The EduProtocol Field Guide* by Marlena Hebern and Jon Corippo
- *The EduProtocol Field Guide: Book 2* by Marlena Hebern and Jon Corippo
- *Instant Relevance* by Denis Sheeran
- *LAUNCH* by John Spencer and A.J. Juliani
- *Make Learning MAGICAL* by Tisha Richmond
- *Pure Genius* by Don Wettrick
- *The Revolution* by Darren Ellwein and Derek McCoy
- *Shift This!* by Joy Kirr
- *Spark Learning* by Ramsey Musallam
- *Sparks in the Dark* by Travis Crowder and Todd Nesloney
- *Table Talk Math* by John Stevens
- *The Wild Card* by Hope and Wade King
- *The Writing on the Classroom Wall* by Steve Wyborney

INSPIRATION, PROFESSIONAL GROWTH, & PERSONAL DEVELOPMENT

- *Be REAL* by Tara Martin
- *Be the One for Kids* by Ryan Sheehy
- *Creatively Productive* by Lisa Johnson
- *Educational Eye Exam* by Alicia Ray
- *The EduNinja Mindset* by Jennifer Burdis
- *Empower Our Girls* by Lynmara Colón and Adam Welcome

- *Finding Lifelines* by Andrew Grieve and Andrew Sharos
- *The Four O'Clock Faculty* by Rich Czyz
- *How Much Water Do We Have?* by Pete and Kris Nunweiler
- *P Is for Pirate* by Dave and Shelley Burgess
- *A Passion for Kindness* by Tamara Letter
- *The Path to Serendipity* by Allyson Apsey
- *Sanctuaries* by Dan Tricarico
- *The SECRET SAUCE* by Rich Czyz
- *Shattering the Perfect Teacher Myth* by Aaron Hogan
- *Stories from Webb* by Todd Nesloney
- *Talk to Me* by Kim Bearden
- *Teach Better* by Chad Ostrowski, Tiffany Ott, Rae Hughart, and Jeff Gargas
- *Teach Me, Teacher* by Jacob Chastain
- *TeamMakers* by Laura Robb and Evan Robb
- *Through the Lens of Serendipity* by Allyson Apsey
- *The Zen Teacher* by Dan Tricarico

CHILDREN'S BOOKS
- *Beyond Us* by Aaron Polansky
- *Cannonball In* by Tara Martin
- *Dolphins in Trees* by Aaron Polansky
- *I Want to Be a Lot* by Ashley Savage
- *The Princes of Serendip* by Allyson Apsey
- *Zom-Be a Design Thinker* by Amanda Fox

ABOUT THE AUTHOR

Diana Gill is an English teacher turned instructional technology coach turned director of technology. She has also served as an innovation specialist for the Indiana Department of Education. She is passionate about supporting educators and has worked to support technology coaches specifically in her state through the Connected Coach Collaborative. She is also a board member for Indiana Connected Educators—an ISTE affiliate. Currently, she serves ISTE as President-Elect of the Online and Blended Learning Network. She is also a proud Google Innovator from #WDC17.

Diana is a foodie but usually sustains herself with pistachios and black tea with honey. She loves to read: mostly historical fiction and Stephen King. She also enjoys running for its meditative and self-competitive qualities. She lives in Northwest Indiana with her husband, Brian, her daughter, McKenna, her son, Ryker, and an entire zoo of dogs.

Made in the USA
Middletown, DE
13 August 2020